THE BOYS' AND GIRLS' BOOK OF
FILMS AND TELEVISION

A

OTHER TITLES IN THE SERIES:

THE BOYS' BOOK OF ASTRONOMY
THE BOYS' BOOK OF BUSES OF THE WORLD
THE BOYS' BOOK OF THE EARTH BENEATH US
THE BOYS' BOOK OF ENGINEERING WONDERS OF THE WORLD
THE BOYS' BOOK OF HOW THINGS ARE MADE
THE BOYS' BOOK OF MAGIC
THE BOYS' BOOK OF MEDICAL SCIENCE
THE BOYS' BOOK OF MODEL RAILWAYS
THE BOYS' BOOK OF MODERN SCIENTIFIC WONDERS
THE BOYS' BOOK OF MOTORS
THE BOYS' BOOK OF THE NAVY
THE BOYS' BOOK OF OUTDOOR LIFE
THE BOYS' BOOK OF POPULAR HOBBIES
THE BOYS' BOOK OF RADIO, TELEVISION AND RADAR
THE BOYS' BOOK OF ROCKS AND FOSSILS
THE BOYS' BOOK OF SAILING
THE BOYS' BOOK OF SCOTLAND YARD
THE BOYS' BOOK OF SPACE
THE BOYS' BOOK OF VETERAN CARS
THE BOYS' BOOK OF WORLD AIRLINES
THE BOYS' BOOK OF WORLD RAILWAYS
THE WINTER BOOK FOR BOYS
THE YOUNG COLLECTOR'S BOOK

THE GIRLS' BOOK OF BALLET
THE GIRLS' BOOK OF BALLROOM DANCING
THE GIRLS' BOOK OF COOKING
THE GIRLS' BOOK OF HORSES AND RIDING
THE GIRLS' BOOK OF OUTDOOR LIFE
THE GIRLS' BOOK OF POPULAR HOBBIES
THE GIRLS' BOOK OF SKATING
THE WINTER BOOK FOR GIRLS

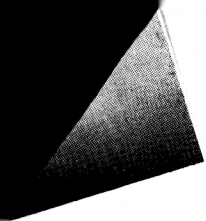

THE BOYS' AND GIRLS' BOOK OF
FILMS AND TELEVISION

MARY FIELD and MAUD MILLER
in association with
ROGER MANVELL

BURKE ⓑ LONDON

ACKNOWLEDGEMENTS

The Author and Publishers wish to thank the following for permission to reproduce photographs and line drawings:

ABC Television Ltd., Associated Television Ltd., The BBC, The British Film Agency, The British Film Institute, Cinema Exhibitors London Ltd., The Czech Government Film Industry, Ealing Studios, The Film Producers Guild, The French Government Tourist Office, The Kodak Museum, The Mansell Collection, Mobile Foto Service, The National Film Archive, The National Film Library, Natural Vision Studios Ltd., Philips Company, The Radio Times Hulton Picture Library, RKO Radio Pictures Ltd., J. Arthur Rank (Productions) Ltd., Rank Precision Industries Ltd., The Science Museum, Shell Film Unit, Studio Vale, *The Times*, A. Traverso, Twentieth Century Fox, C. A. S. Williams.

Burke Publishing Company Ltd.,
14 John Street, London, W.C.1.
Printed in Great Britain by
C. Tinling & Co. Ltd., Liverpool, London and Prescot

Contents

CHAPTER   PAGE

I   COMMUNICATION BY PICTURE   9

II   THE HOW AND WHY OF FILM-MAKING   16

III   THE SILENT YEARS: 1895–1928   43

IV   THE SOUND FILM: 1928–1955   63

V   THE DOCUMENTARY AND THE SHORT FILM   81

VI   HOW TELEVISION WORKS   98

VII   JOHN LOGIE BAIRD   106

VIII   HOW PROGRAMMES REACH THE TELEVISION SCREEN   114

IX   THE FILM IN THE AGE OF TELEVISION   130

X   TYPES OF PROGRAMMES: CINEMA AND TELEVISION   135

XI   THE EFFECTS OF TELEVISION ON THE CINEMA   140

CHAPTER I

Communication by Picture: Films and Television

SOMETIMES WE tend to think of films and television as being new discoveries made during the last sixty years. But really they are only the logical developments of centuries of scientific work, especially in the fields of electricity and of physics. Neither of these great means of communication are the work of one man. Scientists all over the world, working independently, have gradually added pieces to the jigsaw of knowledge. This has been arranged to produce first films and now television.

Men have always tried to communicate with each other by pictures. The earliest forms of writing were pictures which soon became set into symbols that were easy to draw. Chinese writing, for example, started by being pictures and then turned into calligraphy. Ancient Egyptian writing consisted of the same type of stylised pictures, as did the different kinds of writing in Central America used among the native peoples who were there when the Spanish and Portuguese discovered the New World. Our own alphabet is largely based on pictures too, though they are difficult to recognise in our modern writing.

Telling Stories in Pictures

But pictures that remained recognisable pictures have always been the easiest way of giving information or of telling stories to people who cannot read or write or who speak a different language. The earliest drawings of this kind are still to be found on the walls of caves in Southern Europe and North Africa. They show hunting scenes and battles and perhaps stories of the gods and goddesses these primitive people worshipped. They are believed to be magic pictures painted to make the artist and his tribe successful in hunting and in battle. But they do tell stories too—of great hunts and famous battles and of the life, dress and behaviour of the people who worshipped in the caves. They told stories that were handed down from father to son, so that the events on which they were based were not forgotten. Now, after 6,000 years, we can still understand some of the things these prehistoric men were saying in their paintings and can imagine, to some extent, how they lived.

The habit of painting on walls has been followed by more modern people. The Romans had stories painted on the walls of their houses. Tapestries of the Middle Ages tell wonderful stories in needlework —one of the most famous series being the Bayeux Tapestries, which relate the story of the Norman Conquest of England. Churches had stories from the Bible and from the lives of the saints painted on the walls and, more dramatic still, the religious men of nine hundred or a thousand years ago carved stories in stone. You can see some of them in the churchyards of

MODERN FORM	GRADUAL EVOLUTION	EARLIEST FORM	MEANING
象	象 象 象 象 象 象 象	象	Elephant
虎	虎 虎 虎 虎 虎 虎 虎	虎	Tiger

The evolution of Chinese calligraphy

Brittany, where the best-known stories of the Bible are carved on stone Calvaries. In other churches the stories are carved inside; the scenes round the Chapter House at Salisbury must have thrilled the people who looked at them while a priest reminded them of the well-known tales.

Then people of some wealth—but not rich enough to afford tapestries—began to want picture stories in their homes too. Only a few years ago, when the whitewash was taken off the walls of a fourteenth-

A primitive cave drawing

A section of the Bayeux tapestry

century house which had been used by fire-watchers during the war, some of the earliest of these domestic pictures were discovered. They show the birds and animals which lived in the woods and marshes round about. They tell, in pictures, about the seven ages of man, of which Shakespeare wrote nearly two hundred years later in *As You Like It*, and there, with the whitewash cleaned away from above, you can still see the infant "mewling and puking" and the school-boy. By the door is an old legend of the Three Dead Kings. Perhaps, in winter, when the logs flickered in the wide fireplace, the dancing fire-light made the drawings of The Three Kings seem to move, and perhaps the boys and girls in the room were delightfully frightened by the figures that swayed and turned and looked directly at them. They enjoyed, even then, the thrill of moving pictures.

We should remember, too, that even today pictures are used as a way of conveying information. Many people today still read with difficulty and many of us cannot understand the language of the country we are in; London Transport has pictures of how to stop a bus and hotels have pictures by the bells in their bed-rooms, so that it is easy to distinguish which bell to ring for the waiter to bring

food or the chambermaid to make the bed or the porter to fetch your luggage. If you keep your eyes open, you will find plenty of examples of people communicating with you by pictures.

The First Moving Pictures

But all these pictures are *still* pictures. The tapestry swaying in the wind and the wall pictures flickering in the fire-light only seemed to be alive. Men have always longed for pictures which would really move.

Deep in the history of China are records of shadow-shows which made moving pictures on the walls. Such shows are still popular in the Far East. Leonardo da Vinci, who lived in Italy some five hundred years ago and who was both an artist and a scientist, tried to solve problems of light in relation to moving objects. Then again, in the seventeenth century, Athanasius Kircher—a Jesuit priest—made a magic lantern. Although this was a still picture, painted on glass and placed in front of a light so that it was reflected on a wall opposite, it is an important step towards the invention of moving pictures, for it proved that pictures could be projected by a light behind them. People who saw these magic lantern pictures at that time found them as entertaining as we

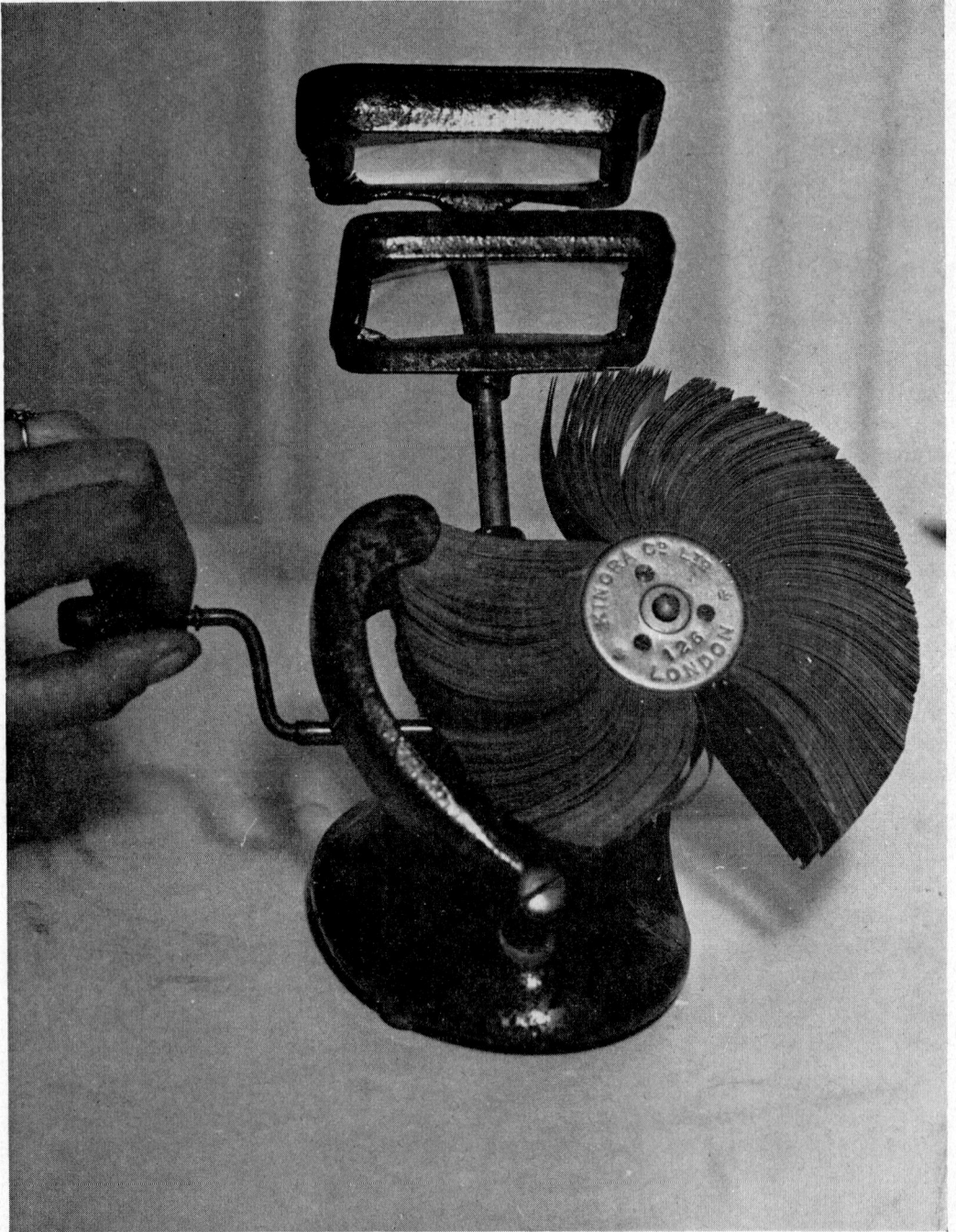

The Kinora picture-viewing machine, mounted on a stand with an adjustable lens. This worked on the flip-book principle

The Praxinoscope—a forerunner of the cinema. With the aid of a candle, mirror and hood, it showed moving bands printed in colour

There was a long gap in the history of moving pictures and then, in 1824, Dr. Peter Mark Roget addressed the Royal Society in London on "The Persistence of Vision with regard to Moving Objects". In simple language, this means that, if you see one picture after another in rapid succession, you carry on your remembrance from one to the next so that they seem to be one picture that changes as it moves, rather than a series of pictures. An experiment which illustrates this can easily be carried out. Make a little book and draw a simple picture in the bottom right-hand corner of each page. Then bend the book back and let the pages flick over very quickly. The persistence of vision will make the series of drawings look like one moving picture.

Some people nowadays do not entirely accept Roget's theory. But, from 1800 to 1850, little books like this were very popular and all kinds of machines were invented to give the illusion of pictures in motion. They would seem like toys to us today, but over a hundred years ago they aroused great interest and had important-sounding names like the Traumatrope,

find today's film-strips. Film-strips are really based on the same principle as the magic lantern show of 1646, the only difference being that the coloured pictures which we see are designed on film and not on glass.

These pictures are part of a Zoetrope slip. Each illustration progressively displays a fractional movement. When seen in quick succession they give the illusion of a moving picture

The Heliocinograph (another type of early viewing machine) in which a slotted shutter is separated from the figure disc but mounted on the same spindle

the Praxinoscope, the Zoëtrope and the Daedalum.

D. A. Spencer and H. D. Waley have written in their book, *The Cinema Today*:

"In order to present any series of pictures to the eye with the illusion that their contents move, it is essential to render invisible the sliding into position and the

The Matagraph projector with a lamp-house. This was in use at the end of the last century

sliding out of position of each picture. This is a matter of some difficulty, because the eye, evolved as an early-warning device in countless generations of animals and men, is extremely sensitive, both to the starting into movement of stationary objects and the sudden stopping of moving ones. . . . The brain . . . has evolved along lines which cause it to overlook . . . brief gaps, provided they are periods of darkness."

The early moving-picture machines were nearly all based on the same idea, which was to paint a series of figures on a cylinder and then twirl the cylinder round. A metal band, pierced with slits, moved outside the cylinder in the opposite direction. This meant that each picture was seen through a slit for a fraction of a second only—and seemed to be part of a single, moving picture.

Films and television programmes of animated cartoons which we see today are very like these early moving pictures of the Zoëtrope. They too are produced by a series of pictures, though nowadays the drawings are more complicated.

But pictures, drawn or painted, could only give a very brief illusion of movement. Pictures which move for a long period of time had to await the invention of photography, which—as we know it—began in 1839.

1839 is not even a hundred and fifty years ago. We are apt to think that the last fifty years are the great years of invention, but all modern inventions are based on the work of scientists who had no idea where their researches were leading. There would have been no films or television today if the Greeks had not turned their minds to mathematics over 2,500 years ago.

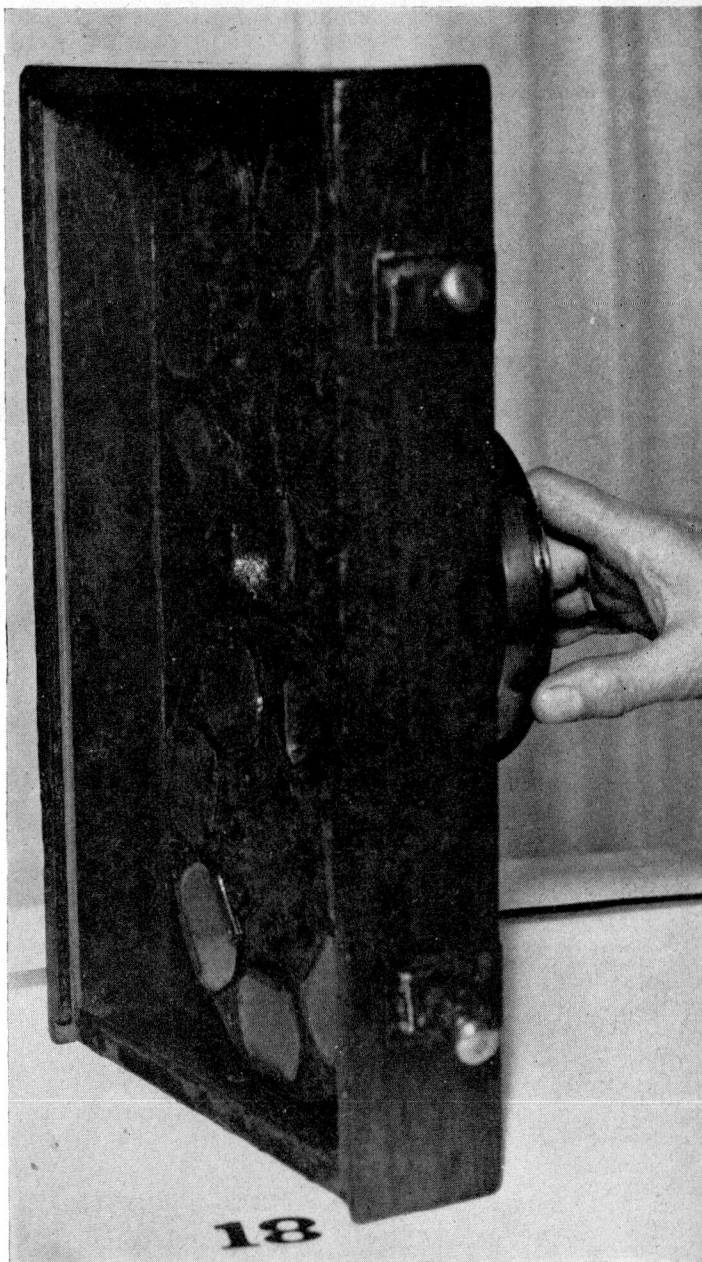

The Bio-phantoscope, by means of which successive pictures were shown, alternating from one disc to the next, giving an illusion of movement

CHAPTER II

The How and Why of Film-making

THE MOTION picture exercises an hypnotic hold on its audience. This is one form of hypnosis resulting from concentration on movement created inside a limited and static area. It is the fascination of the shadow-theatres, or even the simpler joys of hand-made shadows (the laughing donkey who might be a rabbit) and the weirdly dancing match-stick creatures of the flip-books and wheels.

The physical make-up of the cinematographic motion picture can be described as briefly as follows:

The Illusion of the Moving Picture

The picture on the screen appears to the audience to move owing to the persistence of vision. Provided the speed with which the single images follow each other exceeds a certain minimum, the eye sees them as one image in continuous motion. The screen is blanked while one image is removed and replaced by the next, but the eye holds on to the vanished image for a fraction of time sufficient to link it satisfactorily to the next slightly different image.

This illusion of motion was satisfactorily achieved at the rate of sixteen images a second in the days of the silent film. When sound was added to the cinema, it was found necessary for the sake of the sound-track to increase the number of images flashed on to the screen to twenty-four per second. To reproduce natural speed on the screen, the rate of exposure of the camera and the projector must be the same: to achieve the effect of slow-motion, it is necessary to photograph a moving object more quickly than the images will subsequently be projected. For example, the wings of a humming-bird photographed at some hundreds of images per second will be plainly visible in every detail of their movement when the images are projected at normal speed. To achieve the effect of quick-motion, it is necessary to photograph a moving object more slowly than the images will subsequently be projected. (For example, a flower opening its petals to the sun may take an hour to do this in actuality, but these beautiful movements may be shown on the screen in fifteen seconds of quickened motion.) But whatever variants of the rule may be introduced for special reasons, the phenomenon of persistence of vision makes the process of motion picture photography possible.

Background and Title	Organ music ends.		

FADE OUT

| | | 39 | 1 |

FADE IN

3. L.S. Big Ben and Houses of
   Parliament.

   Traffic starts.

   CUT TO:

   Commentary starts:
   TIM: My name is Tim,
   Tim Smith, and I live   7   15
   in London. This is
   the story of a holiday

4. L.S. High angle looking down
   on to pedestrian crossing.

   I once had in Holland.

   CUT TO: 6   10

5. L.S. Busy street in London.
   A Little Old Lady walks
   slowly towards camera.

   . . . and although I
   didn't know it at the
   time, it was here, in
   London, that the story
   really began.

   CUT TO: 8   8

6. M.S. Old Lady stops by the
   window of Jewel shop, then
   totters o.s. right as Motor-
   cyclist walks towards camera
   and also stops by window and
   looks in at jewellery.

   Music starts.

   CUT TO: 12   7

7. M.S. Camera shooting through
   shop window from inside on
   to cyclist, with Old Lady in
   b.g. right of screen. Motor-
   cyclist looks furtively round
   then pulls goggles down over
   his eyes and takes brick out
   of jacket and throws it at   Smash of glass.
   window. He then exits shot   Alarm bell.
   rapidly screen right.

                                     OLD LADY: Oh, Oh!
                                     Help! Police! Stop
                                     that man! . . .

   CUT TO: 12   12

The first section of the Children's Film Foundation script for the film Hunted in Holland. *The preparation of the film script is the first stage in transforming an idea into a film. Note the details of camera movement. In a television script, by contrast, the camera is the concern of the director on the set*

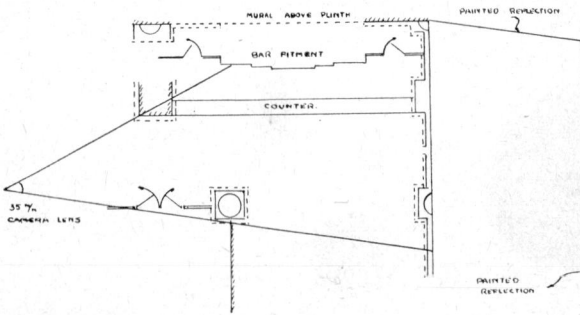

MURAL ABOVE PLINTH   PAINTED REFLECTION

BAR FITMENT

COUNTER

35 ⁿ/ₘ
CAMERA LENS

PAINTED
REFLECTION

Set design: Above: *The artist's original design.* Left: *The plan for the set, showing camera position and the general layout.* Below: *The set when constructed*

Once the set has been designed, as the result of the doodles of the art director which gradually turn into scene sketches, set drawings and scale models (above), the finished model is checked for lighting and camera positions (below). Note the perspective and detail drawings and a copy of the shooting script pinned to the shelves

*While the art director is design-
ing the sets, the costume designer
plans the clothes which are then
the responsibility of the wardrobe
department*

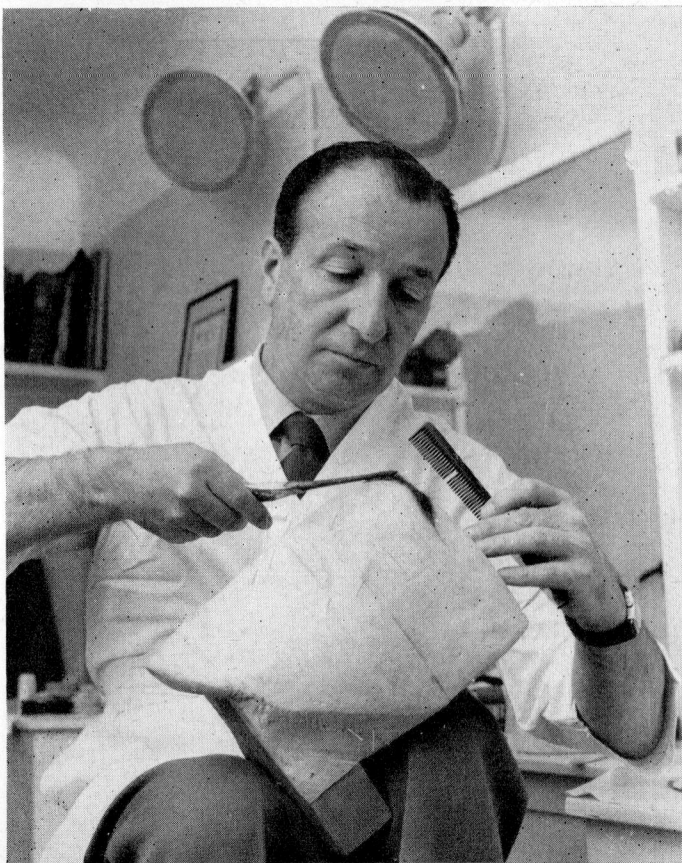

*Alongside the plans for costumes
to be worn by the actors, the
make-up experts are busy and the
staff of the hair-dressing department are at work on such jobs as
making waves in a toupee to be
worn by one of the leading actors*

The behind-the-scenes pre-parations for a film set include the carpenters' careful construction work

Sometimes the practical requirements of the film are unusual but they never prove too difficult for the versatile staff of the film company, even if they are called upon to produce a larger-than-life, imposing "stone" statue

Often one small shot may involve a tremendous amount of work and enormous expense. This set for Destination Unknown *demanded a camera crane, a 50,000 dollar ship, special lighting and other equipment*

It is essential, if the filming is to be successful, that the positioning of lights is carefully plotted and that these plots are followed

Special effects may even include giving nature a hand. For sea sequences in one film "rain-makers" provided fifty square yards of cloud-burst

When on location it may be necessary to obtain the correct lighting effects by the use of reflectors

Whether the film is a simple one involving little in the way of special sets or props, or whether it is a great spectacle demanding a cast of thousands and many location shots, the camera, in some shape or form, is ready to record it all on celluloid

SUNSHADE CLAMP RING LOCK SCREW
SOLID MATTE
GAUZE FRAME
GAUZE FRAME KNOBS
3 INCH FILTER FRAME KNOB
LEATHER BELLOWS
2 INCH FILTER FRAME KNOB
SUNSHADE
SOLID MATTE
GAUZE FRAME
NEWALL C.538
POLA SCREEN LOCK SCREW
MATTE RAIL BRACKET LOCKING SCREW
BELLOWS EXTENSION CLAMP SCREW
MATTE LOCK SCREW
RISING FRONT LOCK SCREW
HORIZONTAL SLIDE BRACKET
BELLOWS EXTENSION CLAMP SCREW
MATTE RAIL EXTENSION TUBE
MATTE RAIL EXTENSION TUBE LOCK SCREW

Details of the matte box and sunshade of the film camera. In the matte box are incorporated holders for filters, diffusion discs, gauze slides and a pola screen

The camera mounted on a geared head, in turn mounted on a geared dolly. This enables almost any combination of tracking, panning, sweeping and rising to be achieved

UPPER
SPROCKET
GUIDE

SPROCKET

BUCKLE
TRIP
PLATE

LOWER
SPROCKET
GUIDE

BUCKLE TRIP
RESET KNOB

The camera box into which is fitted a circular housing carrying the main bearings for the sprocket shaft

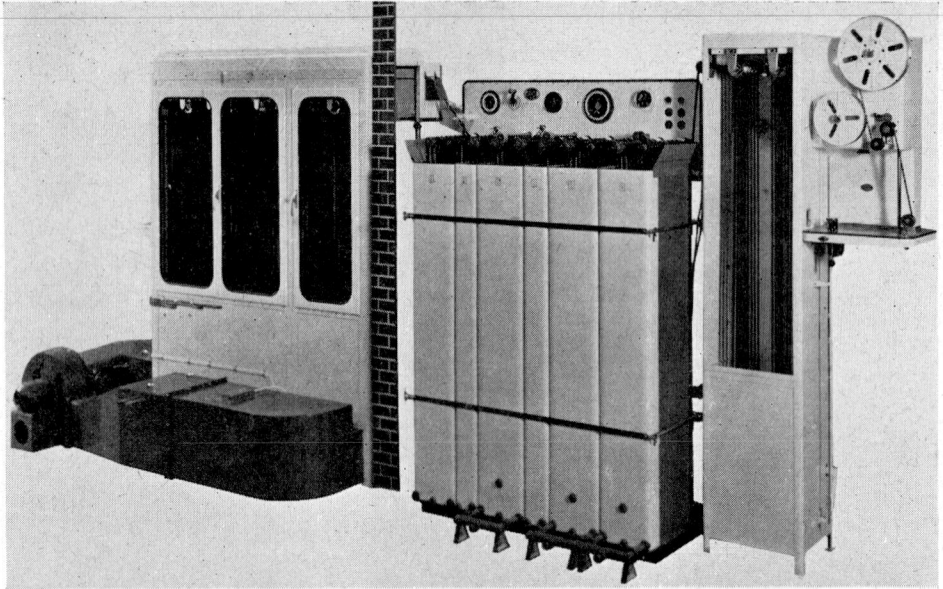

The film taken by the camera is fed, on a spool, through a series of vertical tanks for developing, washing, fixing and final washing. This latter end of the equipment is in complete darkness. The remainder of the machine, beyond the indicated brick wall is the drying section and is fed with warm air from the blower system

When the film is developed the editor works on his cutting copy to produce the final version. Here is a film editing machine with which the cutting is done. Alongside it is the cut film, ready for rejoining in correct sequence

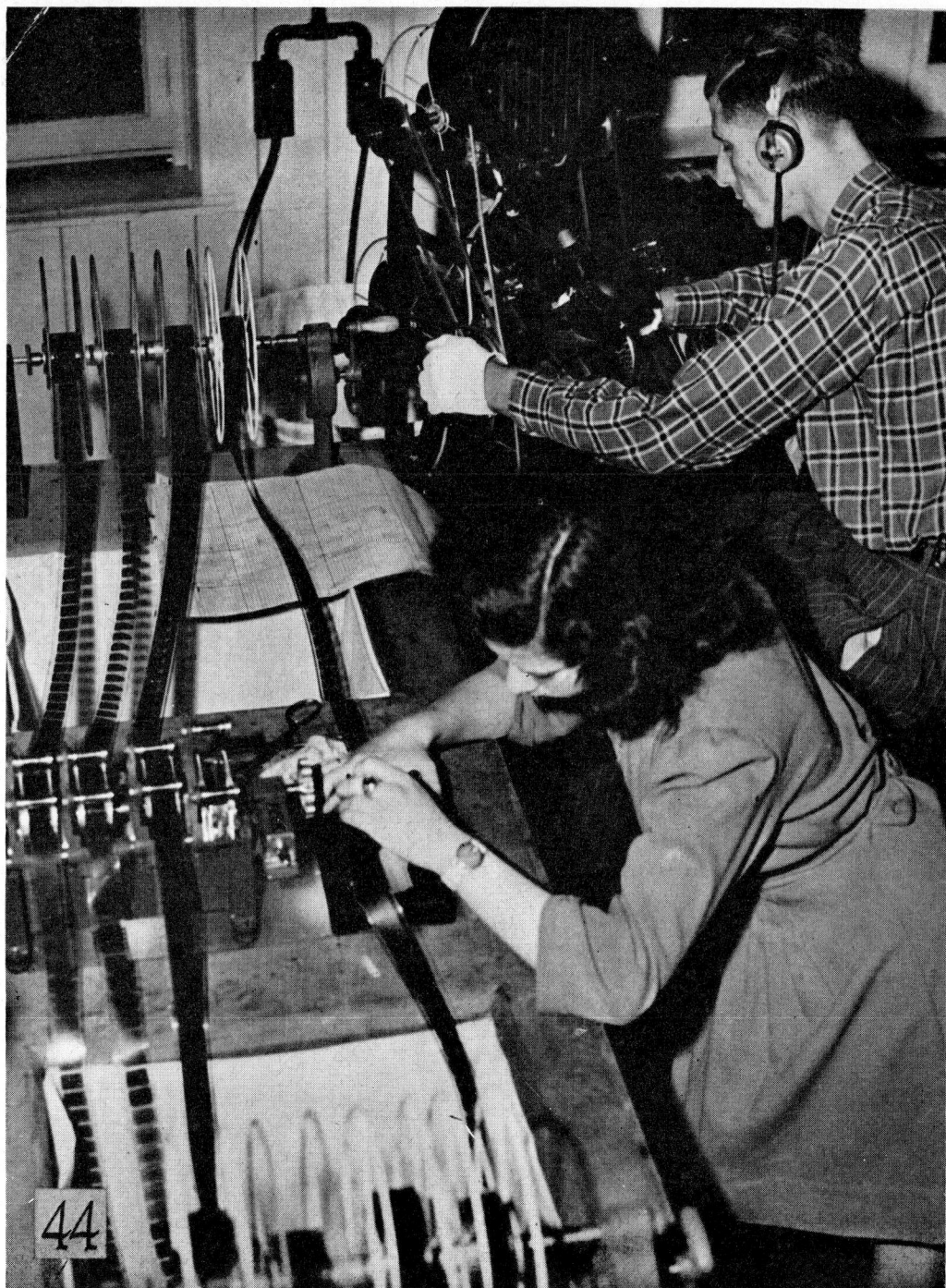

The cutting room in which different tracks are spliced, checked for correct length and synchronised with one another

Sound plays a major part in today's films. It is the job of the editor to get both sound and picture into the right form. One man who helps to provide the sound is the effects man who has more than one hundred instruments in his one-man band

The optical sound camera which transfers magnetic (or taped) sound on to film

A magnetic and optical sound projector

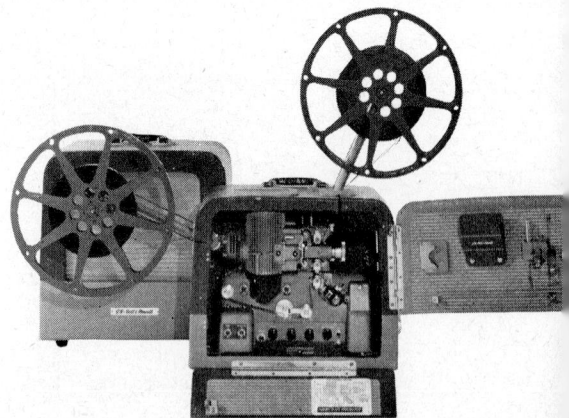

The recording engineer is a difficult man to please. His delicate apparatus is far more sensitive to sound than the most sensitive human ear

A re-recording mixing console with eight inputs which is used to combine a number of separate sound tracks, such as dialogue, music and sound effects. It is housed in a viewing theatre—the screen can be seen at the right—in which a microphone is provided to facilitate the recording of a commentary

Adjacent to the viewing theatre is a projection room. This view of it shows a picture and sound projector, with amplifier cabinets behind it. The projection room is also equipped with three sound track reproducers and other apparatus used for reproducing sound from gramophone records or from magnetic tape. The sound outputs of these machines are fed to the mixer console shown previously

In the recording theatre the chief sound engineer sits at his controls, waiting for the "silent" film to start running

The "silent" film is projected by this apparatus. The projectors can be adapted for all types of film, including wide-screen and CinemaScope

When the film is finally complete it is projected on to your local cinema screen by a projector like this one

The Celluloid: Its Length and Speed in Projection

The images themselves are reproduced on a continuous band of celluloid coated with emulsion sensitive to light. Initially, the negative film is exposed in the motion-picture camera. Subsequently, it is subjected to the normal photographic processes before a positive print is produced from it. The combination of hundreds of shots each composed of hundreds of single images on the band of celluloid makes up the finished film. Photographed and projected at twenty-four images a second, it takes 14,400 separate images to make a ten-minute film. This would cover nearly a thousand feet of standard-width 35-mm. film. (Film also exists in other gauges, ranging from Todd-AO's 70 mm. down to 8 mm. used by amateurs.)

Photographed Sound: the Illusion of Sound and Image

The sound is reproduced photographically as a light-band, known as the sound-track, printed alongside the images on the celluloid film. As the sound is reproduced through a loud-speaker normally placed behind the screen, the audience associates it directly with the motion picture itself. This is useful for the film-maker, because a great deal of film-making depends on the crude or the subtle association of sounds with objects and persons that could never produce them. For example, a beautiful actress may not be able to sing, but this does not matter, since her lip-movements can be matched to a sound-track recorded by an ugly but well-voiced soprano: the audience then has the benefit of both beauty and song. Most films nowadays have the greater part of their

Compare the conventional 35-mm. film (left) with the 70-mm. film used in the Todd-AO system (right). In addition, whilst standard film normally accommodates one optical sound track, the 70-mm. film has six magnetic tracks

Careful positioning of the camera produces a deliberate distortion which achieves dramatic effect. In this picture, with the dog so emphatically positioned in the foreground, the man seems to be irresistibly drawn towards the dog, a point very necessary to the climax of Across the Bridge

sound recorded at a different time from the shooting of the picture: this is known as post-synchronisation and allows ideally-recorded sound to be matched with ideally-photographed images—or so the theory goes. But the audience, psychologically speaking, is prepared to accept the illusion that sound and image belong to one and the same phenomenon reproduced for them in the cinema.

The Illusory Third Dimension

The image the audience sees on the screen is a two-dimensional one: it has height and width, but no depth. The cinema, for all its appearance of actuality, is only an illusion of light and shadow. Yet so advanced are the photographic processes, both in black and white and in colour, that the audience willingly lends perspective to the shadows on the screen. Possessing two eyes, the normal human being perceives the part of the world within his field of vision from a dual viewpoint. These views are merged in the brain to form a picture which appears to have the spatial depth that we know the physical environment around us does indeed possess. It is much more easy to move about a room crowded with furniture or a street crowded with moving traffic if we have the advantage of this bifocal vision.

The world of spatial depth has, however, aesthetic potentialities different from those of a two-dimensional picture. It may be more accurate to say that these aesthetic potentialities have a greater complexity rather than that they are essentially different. This is, however, a very important distinction, and one which places the motion-picture inside the limited sphere of art as distinct from the relatively uncontrolled experience of actuality itself. To the bifocally-visioned human being the world is three-dimensional, whereas the motion-picture image is two-dimensional. The perspective of depth which we rapidly learn to supply, as a result of our normal experience, is a kindly illusion. We see a room on the screen, and we at once proceed to give it the quality of visual depth which, in fact, it cannot possess.

Mobile Composition of the Film

A film, then, consists of a large number of two-dimensional projected photographs capable of creating the illusion of being a single continuous moving photograph. The units of which it is made up are called cine-frames, the individual photographs on the celluloid band. These combine together to make a single moving shot, or scene, which the camera takes either from a set viewpoint or whilst it is itself moved about during the shot. The group of shots which, combined together, make up a completed phase in the whole story is collectively called a sequence. A scene or shot is like an illustrated sentence or even a short paragraph in the story: the sequence is like a chapter.

Each shot watches the action from a selected viewpoint, near or far away. If each shot were immobile, the laws of composition governing still photography would operate, and the story would be told like a strip cartoon or a magic-lantern slide series. But each shot is mobile, and therefore the laws of mobile composition, a new and unique art form, operate. This mobile composition is governed by two factors, the *shape* of the movement inside the frame and the *time* that movement takes. This factor of shape is, like still composition, partly governed by its

A scene from London Films' production, Anna Karenina. *The lighting and positioning of the camera both help to achieve the overwhelming atmosphere of this studio scene*

relation to the surrounding boundaries of the screen-frame; the movement, however, produces its own pictorial climax. Each shot in a well-calculated film moves towards something—that is, achieves a step forward in the story as well as a step forward in the total movement of the film, just as a bar of music contributes to the total development of a symphony.

Mobile composition is, therefore, a rhythmic pictorial movement which reinforces by its shape and timing the action of the scene played. For example, a girl descends a staircase thinking that the man in the hall below is her lover. She runs down lightly, her long dress flowing behind her. At the foot of the staircase she stops suddenly, her hand gripping the bole of the balustrade, her dress flowing forward and swinging back with the shock of her sudden stillness. It is not her lover, but her enemy. He moves forward into the frame, so that we see the back of his head and left shoulder: his movement into the picture is complementary to her lack of movement; the gay flow of her dress is superseded by the shock of its swinging to a significant stillness. Owing to the curious and special laws of perspective in the motion picture the little figure of the girl, which began its movement downstairs from the top right-hand corner of the frame, becomes the big figure which dominates the picture once she stops, because the camera has been so placed that her last action, the sudden stop with her hand on the balustrade, forms the most emphatic, the boldest piece of composition in the whole scene: the bole of the balustrade is in the foreground, and the *scale* of the girl changes from insignificant to dominant as she comes down into the foreground of the picture. Were this scene to take place in real life, observed bifocally with the human eye instead of through the single eye of

C

A shot from ground level produces the required distortion in the scene from a Russian film, Peter the Great, *seen from this angle, the leader appears as a dominant figure, towering over his men*

words, camera-position in relation to the actors in a scene can achieve a psychological composition which the audience accepts at a glance without the need for verbal interpretation. "You are in my power", "I love you" or "I hate you" can be expressed by mobile composition alone.

Colour and Light Values

You will notice, in the cinema, that a few minutes after the start of a well-made film its mood and atmosphere will have been established not only in terms of composition, but in terms of its photographic values. Many film directors of imagination, such as D. W. Griffith and Sergei Eisenstein, habitually worked with the same cameraman, who understood how to paint (as it were) their colleagues' emotions in the light and shade or the colour values of motion picture photography.

It is wrong to speak of colour photog-

the camera, the *scale* of the girl's body would not seem to change as she comes nearer to the observer. But because this movement is reproduced on a two-dimensional plane, the viewer can only partially compensate *psychologically* for this movement in depth, and the girl consequently changes her scale as she moves into the chosen foreground of the picture. This play with perspectives, with visual dominances and emphases, is a continual process in the mobile composition of the individual shot in a well-calculated film.

Many a shot in films made during the past quarter-century have used this comparative loss of perspective relationship to place a dominating figure in the foreground of the cine-frame in strong contrast to some dwarfed figure in the background of the picture, the bully seeming to tower over his victim, both visually and psychologically. In other

A close-up from D. W. Griffith's masterpiece, Intolerance (1916). *No more expressive picture could be made to reveal a wife's emotion during her husband's trial for murder*

raphy as if it were totally different from black-and-white photography instead of an extension of it to include other colour values. Black-and-white photography has reached a high level in the subtlety of its suggestion of atmosphere. The black-and-white film is, in effect, a conventional limitation of colour range which we have come to accept and which has achieved great flexibility.

In black-and-white photography the question of interpretation always arises. Its emphasis of light and shade, its stress of strong highlight and deep shadow can in itself create the mood for melodrama, tragedy or gaiety. The mobile composition of a film often requires the exploitation of the dancing play of light and darkness, as, for example, the sunlight falling through leaves or flashing on lapping water, or moonlight softly revealing the shapes of a village street. It can suggest menace by the penetration of its shadows and the part they play in the composition of the scene.

Colour, however, in itself possesses powers of suggestion outside the limitations of the purely black-and-white film. By its greater variety it helps the spectator to create the illusion of the third dimension.

Foreground cactus, silhouetted rider, details of plants and grasses all contribute to the artistry of this scenic shot from a film called The Bandit

The sheer lambasting on the screen of all the colour values at once is like over-eating when you are hungry: the eye laps up the colour to the point of satiety. On the other hand, colour can alter the whole interpretation of a strange experience.

Many people were puzzled about the reason for using colour in *Scott of the Antarctic* until they saw the film and discovered a new vision of what they had imagined to be the most colourless part of the earth. On the other hand, colour can be used so unostentatiously that many people who have just seen a colour film may not be able to recollect whether it was made in colour or not. The very denial of the right to use colour when it is fully possible to do so may well result in stressing most effectively the sheer absence of colour in the subject—for example in a surburban street on a wet night in November! In other words, colour photography is yet another opportunity for the film-maker to develop the atmosphere and the drama of his subject.

The New Screens

In addition to the so-called normal screens, which are now roughly 1·6 wide to 1 in height, there is also the CinemaScope screen with which most cinemas are equipped and which is well over twice as wide as it is high, varying slightly from cinema to cinema. But in the great battle to win audiences back from television, there have been several developments in the form of special giant-screen systems designed to show films in a strictly limited number of theatres which are chosen as suitable for the installation of the expensive equipment needed to project these unusually large pictures.

The first of these giant-screen systems was Cinerama, which was first shown to the public in New York in 1952. Its vast, curved screen has an aspect ratio of 2·85 to 1, and the picture is made up of three films shown side by side by three projectors which are interlocked so that the three pictures link together to make one. This screen is suitable mainly for the travelogue type of film, for scenic display and

35

spectacle. The second giant-screen system, and one of some importance to the future of the cinema, is Todd-AO, originally sponsored by the late Michael Todd, the film producer, and the American Optical Company. Todd-AO uses a single double-width film, 70 mm. instead of the usual 35 mm., and both camera and projector secure a huge panoramic picture covering an angle of 128°. Todd-AO is eminently well adapted for presenting spectacular productions, such as the musical, *South Pacific*.

The Todd-AO camera showing the large "Bugeye" lens which can sweep and record fully a 128-degree view. The lens mounting is interchangeable and can accommodate three other lenses, 64-, 48-, and 37-degrees

The Todd-AO projector, which uses film 70-mm. wide (double the normal width)

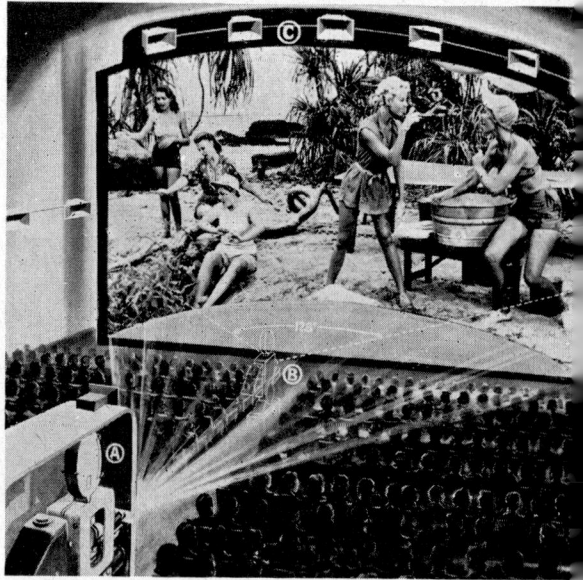

The positioning of the Todd-AO projector eliminates viewing distortion. Special wide-angle lenses create a screen image which could only otherwise be obtained by placing a "phantom" projector (B) in front of the auditorium. Recorded sound, from ninety-six separate sources, is reproduced on six sound channels with high-fidelity loud-speakers positioned above the curved screen, and in the auditorium

Sound

The flexibility of the film medium should now be apparent. Although it has so far been seen at its best when reproducing the visible, natural world around us,

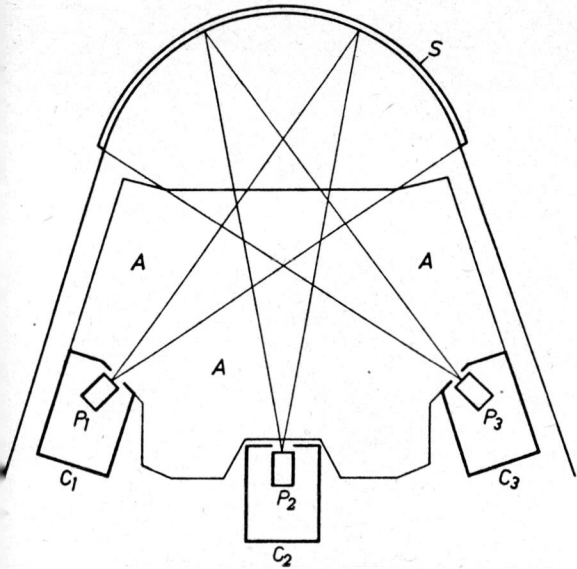

A diagram showing the Cinerama system: S—the screen; P1, P2, P3—the three projectors; C1, C2, C3—the projection rooms; A—the audience

there is no reason at all why it should be confined to presenting actuality. It has, in fact, abandoned naturalism most frequently in its use of sound.

For the most part the sound we hear accompanying a film is recorded entirely separately and at a different time from the photography of the action seen on the screen, except for certain dialogue scenes which happen to be easy to record, technically speaking, at the moment the action is photographed. This opens up the opportunity to develop the sound-track freely in a wholly artificial manner which aims at creating the right artistic effect to supplement, support and even counterpoint the visual image.

The distinguished film director, Thorold Dickinson, in a published discussion, describes as follows the building up of the sound to accompany a short African dance sequence in *Men of Two Worlds*:

"We took recordings in Africa of the sounds of the dances. We found a secret dance society and photographed their dances in notebook shots in daylight. . . . When we came back to London, we collected a lot of dancers and trained them from the notebook shots. . . . But when we came to use the African sound recordings against those studio dances they proved absolutely impossible, because they were all taken from one microphone position, whereas the visual shots of the dancing were taken from several camera positions. The whole thing needed to be an orchestration of sounds, recorded at varying distances from the microphone. The job became one of dealing with the real elements of sound film which are not in the usual way properly exploited. Then all the sounds had to be re-recorded on to one sound track. The final result was entirely cinematic in sound and picture perspective and just could not exist except through the medium of film."

The artist of the film has at his disposal the recorded sounds of Nature, the words and songs of the whole human race, and the music of a single instrument or a combination of instruments. By the interplay of sounds recorded on different separate sound-tracks, he can build up, wholly artificially, a new and final sound-track, and relate it as he wishes to what the audience is seeing on the screen. He can show the effects of words spoken by letting the audience hear them on the sound-track while they watch the reactions of the listeners in close-up. We can watch a silent face on the screen as thoughts are spoken aloud (as in Laurence Olivier's *Hamlet*). We can hear the artificial orchestration of natural sounds, as in the oil-boring sequence in Robert Flaherty's *Louisiana Story*. The film-maker can point the action on the screen by using sound satirically, or by developing it in contrast to the mood of the scene (as in the mocking gaiety or sadness of the zither music in Carol Reed's film, *The Third Man*), or by using it to elicit the inner mood of the action (as, for example, when a distant female voice sings like some remote siren luring the explorers to the Pole in *Scott of the Antarctic*). A hundred different examples of the way sound can be made to supplement and enrich the image on the screen can be discovered by watching the films you see carefully. In fact, the very first sound films of such directors as René Clair and Alfred Hitchcock began to explore these possibilities as soon as the sound-track became available to the film-maker.

The range and quality of sound on film has been immeasurably increased and improved by the introduction of the magnetic striped track on to the film in place of the optical or photographic track. The magnetic stripe is the equivalent of adding the magnetic tape of a tape-recorder to the roll of celluloid; the stripe runs down the side of the picture. The film studios now use magnetic sound recording as much as possible during production. An increasing number of the larger cinemas are being equipped to use this advanced form of sound reproduction, and the more spectacular films have multiple magnetic tracks striped on them that feed different elements in their sound to loudspeakers spaced at different positions behind the giant screen and round the auditorium of the cinema.

Music in Films

The largest chain of concert halls in the world is the cinemas. Here everything is played—from the latest requirements of jazz to the classical repertoire needed for the most recent film biography of a com-

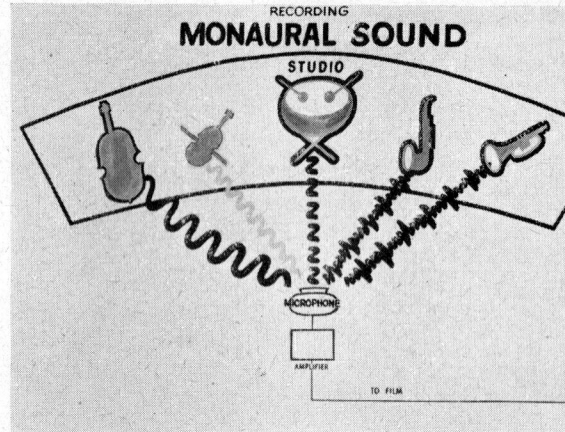

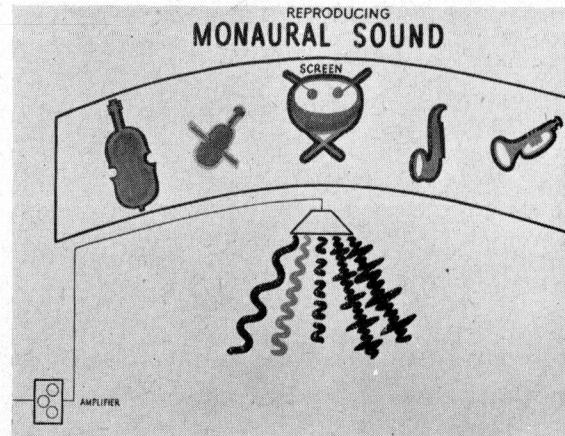

poser or singer. In the period of the silent films the larger cinemas maintained their own "house" orchestras. In the afternoons an indefatigable pianist, with one eye on the screen whilst the other skimmed a thick wad of music sheets, managed to keep her hands going in a steady output of sound which matched, with varying degrees of propriety, the changing moods of the scene. Imaginative film-makers like D. W. Griffith soon learned the importance of trying to control this powerful stimulant to their audience's emotions, and compiled special scores for release with their films. Few people realise that Griffith, like Chaplin today, was by way

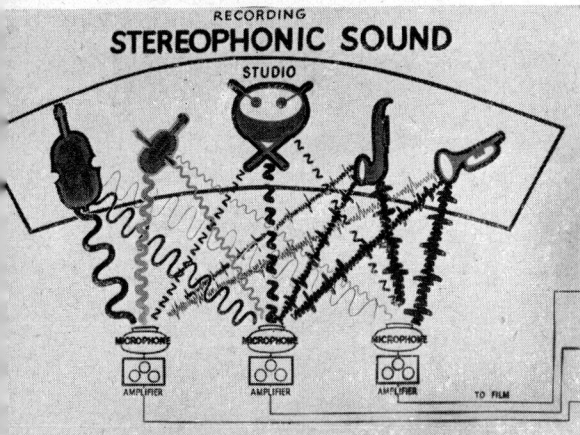

RECORDING
STEREOPHONIC SOUND
STUDIO

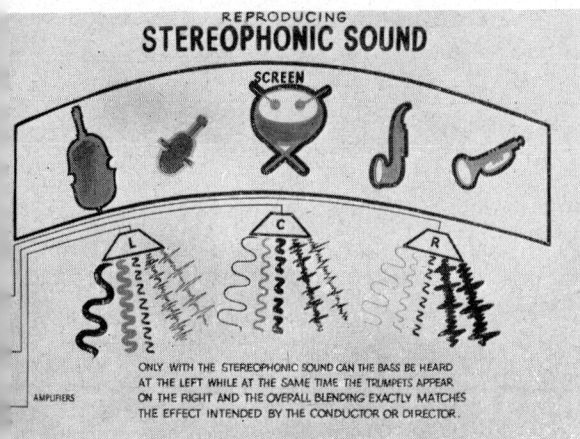

REPRODUCING
STEREOPHONIC SOUND
SCREEN

ONLY WITH THE STEREOPHONIC SOUND CAN THE BASS BE HEARD AT THE LEFT WHILE AT THE SAME TIME THE TRUMPETS APPEAR ON THE RIGHT AND THE OVERALL BLENDING EXACTLY MATCHES THE EFFECT INTENDED BY THE CONDUCTOR OR DIRECTOR.

posers gradually began to appear among the screen credits until (in Britain at least) their presence in the cinema came to be accepted with far too little comment— Bliss, Bax, Vaughan Williams, Walton, Britten, Alwyn, Rawsthorne, Prokoviev, Honegger, Copland, Virgil Thomson. Some composers have expressed themselves with enthusiasm about this exacting work; Vaughan Williams, for example, spoke of it as "splendid discipline", and claimed: "I still believe that the film contains potentialities for the combination of all the arts such as Wagner never dreamed of." Others were disillusioned to find that their work had to be controlled by the stop-watch and only too often made subsidiary to other forms of sound—to dialogue and realistic sound-effects. The composer—creator of the purest of all forms of emotional expression in the arts— had to learn to become a working partner in a studio team; he had to learn a new craft, a rich development of the older craft of composing incidental music for the theatre, such as German, Sullivan, Elgar, Parry, Stanford and Coleridge-Taylor had all been contracted to create for Sir Henry Irving in the previous century.

Music and the Silent Film

In the days of the silent film, albums of musical fragments were published to help the harassed pianist or orchestra leader to follow the film with an increasing stock of conventional pieces to meet all likely demands. The most elaborate collection was that made by an Italian, Giuseppe Becce, in 1919. He compiled a library of musical extracts to fit all moods, carefully timed and catalogued. An experienced film pianist only needed to view a film once or twice in advance of the public performance. He could then weave a pattern of musical sound which dovetailed with both the action and the mood of

of being a composer as well as a film-maker.

The Film Score

When the arrival of the synchronous sound-track put the control of the timing and execution of music directly into the hands of the film-maker, the serious development of the film score as a new branch of composition became possible. The noisy stream of accompanying musical sound developed gradually into the specially composed, carefully timed score, as enlightened film-makers and composers came to terms with each other's art. The names of distinguished com-

what was happening on the screen. In London it has been possible to hear one of the expert pianists of the days of the silent cinema, Arthur Dulay, accompany the silent films which are now constantly being shown at the National Film Theatre.

The natural sounds which are so important in the film today could only rarely be imitated from the orchestra pit of the silent cinema. This meant that the music itself often had to produce effects similar to these natural sounds. In scenes of violence, for example, it was comparatively easy for music to assume the sounds of war, the thunder of cannonade, the martial clash of arms.

The pianist and the orchestra played an all-important part in the silent cinema. But the pioneer of the special score remains D. W. Griffith, whose powerful sense of what made an impressive film led him to devise the most effective music to emphasise the strong emotions underlying the themes of his greatest films, *The Birth of a Nation* and *Intolerance*, shown in 1915 and 1916.

Griffith had studied composition and knew something about music; he composed certain themes himself, but the greater part of the music he used was made up of established themes by such composers as Grieg, Wagner, Beethoven and Tchaikovsky. The cueing for whole sequences and for individual moments of action was most elaborate. How much, I wonder, did this score—made up of so many themes from classical and traditional sources—help the public understand the great potentialities of the cinema which Griffith's films revealed for the first time? When they saw *The Birth of a Nation*, many who had until then thought the cinema a vulgar fairground entertainment realised that they were witnesses to the birth of a new art. The effect of the battle scenes reconstructing the American Civil War, when accompanied by Griffith's musical arrangements, was electrifying. He built up a rhythm in his editing of these scenes, piling up shot upon shot in a crescendo of movement. The vast panoramas looking down on the outstretched lines of the armies half hidden in the smoke from the cannonade were cut in with intimate shots of the men in battle, dying in the no-man's-land of war. And in the orchestra pit below the screen, the dynamic music grew with the picture above, welded into one compulsive whole.

Music and the Sound Film

Composing for the contemporary film is a considerable undertaking for the musician. Some composers in Hollywood devote their lives to this work, and it is only too easy for them to drift into conventions of providing stretches of appropriate "blare" and "blah" against the moving hand of the stop-watch. This is rightly called by the contemptuous term —background music. It is not *functional* music, not music playing a real part in the drama. Examples are perhaps the best way to see how music can be integrated into the dramatic atmosphere and action of a film:

The Sound Barrier (director, David Lean; composer, Malcolm Arnold). At the beginning of the film a pilot in a Spitfire is racing across the sky in the joy of solo flight. The music responds directly to this lyrical feeling. Then the plane plunges into a dive, and begins a mysterious and terrifying buffeting as it approaches the sound barrier. The music changes its nature, and blends with the natural sound of the vibrating plane into a single, tense, dramatic sound effect.

Blithe Spirit (composer, Richard Addinsell). A comic character, a spiritualist medium called Madame Arcati, rides determinedly down a village street on a

Ralph Vaughan Williams, the distinguished composer, listens intently while the music he wrote specially for a film is being played for the recording of a sound-track

bicycle; she passes over a bridge, scattering the ducks, whose peace she destroys with her wavering wheels. A vibraphone suggests her professional link with the ghostly world; the notes of the trumpet call her to duty. The music reflects each phase of her self-propulsion on the bicycle. (Such a close relationship of sight and sound is only achieved in the normal film after it has been photographed, cut and assembled for projection on the screen for the composer to see in as near as possible its final form. He is then given careful and detailed time checks for all the various sections for which it is decided that music is necessary—these ranging from extended phases of some minutes' duration down to the shortest phases of a few seconds only bridging sequences or musical chords required for dramatic emphasis.)

These two examples show something of the variety of tasks set for the composer by the film-maker. The film is best served by composers of distinction (which does not mean the some thing as famous or established composers) who are prepared to give the time and take the trouble to mould their work to the dramatic needs of the picture—and this, of course, includes the other elements on the sound-track, the voices and the natural sounds. Film music exists to reinforce the drama.

41

Therefore the best film music must be *dramatic* music integrated into the action.

Normally the result is music inseparable from the film itself. But sometimes a film score provides themes sufficiently extensive for the music to be arranged for separate performance in its own right through the medium of the concert hall and the gramophone recording. Examples of such scores are Bliss's pioneer composition for *Things to Come* (1935), Prokoviev's music for *Alexander Nevsky*, Walton's music for *Henry V* and *Hamlet*, Virgil Thomson's arrangement of themes derived from folk-music for *Louisiana Story*, and Copland's austerely moving composition for *Our*

Town. Vaughan Williams' score for *Scott of the Antarctic* exists apart from the film in two forms—as a suite of themes and in the symphony *Sinfonia Antarctica* which the composer developed subsequently as a new composition.

Recently it has become possible to obtain recordings of the original sound track of certain films in which the music can be heard in its proper setting of dialogue and sound-effects. The whole of Laurence Olivier's production of *Richard III*, with William Walton's music, is available on gramophone records, and MGM's production of *Julius Caesar* is a wonderfully exciting disc.

A scene from Ealing Studios' production Scott of the Antarctic, *in which the shots of ice and snow were made even more impressive by the music which Vaughan Williams composed to accompany and interpret them*

CHAPTER III

The Silent Years: 1895—1928

The British Feature Film

WE ARE so familiar with the cinema that we easily forget that it has all happened in the lifetime of a man of seventy. We are reminded of this as the centenaries of the pioneers in the invention of the moving picture arrive—the centenaries of their birth, not of their discoveries. In 1955 Britain celebrated the centenary of one of these pioneers, William Friese-Greene, whose name has become something of a legend in the first days of British cinematography.

William Friese-Greene

Friese-Greene is one of the most famous names in this pioneer period. He was a romantic figure, a handsome, volatile man who was a fashionable portrait photographer, but who threw away his fortune because he was obsessed with a desire to produce the necessary apparatus, camera and projector, to make motion pictures. His chief patent was that of June 21, 1889, which outlined his designs for a camera of the so-called "intermittent" type—that is, using a band of film which is held stationary while each image is photographed and obscured when the film is moved on to the next space for the next picture. The patent also described a projector working on a similar intermittent principle. In his pursuit of the technical development of the film as we know it today, Friese-Greene twice bankrupted himself, and lived, lonely and impoverished, to see the collective contributions of other and more prominent inventors and promoters—such as Edison of America and the Lumière family of France—lead to the rapid establishment of a great new international entertainment industry based on motion-picture photography.

Amateur and Professional Pioneers

The true answer to the question of who invented the cinema is that many people contributed to the development—amateur inventors (like R. W. Paul, a London instrument-maker), professional inventors (like Edison in America), professional photographers (like Friese-Greene in England), scientists (like Jules Marey in France) and, of course, businessmen like the French Lumière family, to whom the final credit must be given for developing the film as a commercial form of entertainment on an international scale. Working independently, now one, now another pulled ahead with an idea, a patent, a private demonstration and, finally, a public performance. The cinema as we know it today was the joint invention of them all—the final achievers of the miracle which had lured mankind for centuries, the power to make a picture on a screen which can take on life through the illusion of continuous and natural movement.

FG·CP·95

Robert Donat in a scene from The Magic Box *from the British film on the life of Friese-Greene. The camera shown here is a replica of Friese-Greene's first movie camera*

William Friese-Greene, the British pioneer in cinematography

precious objects of each inventor's care as he examined the first-fruits of his cameras.

Laying the Foundations

It was left to men like the Lumières and Méliès in France, R. W. Paul, George Albert Smith and Cecil Hepworth in Britain and Edwin S. Porter in America to lay the foundations of cinematography in a manner which would appeal to the public and form the basis of both a new art and a new entertainment industry. Of these men, both Hepworth and Smith survived into the nineteen-twenties. Let us take Smith's career as an example. He entered the film industry in 1897, and built a glass studio in some grounds he leased in Brighton. In 1898 he was already beginning to be successful as a film-maker, and was not only shooting newsreels and short-story films but, like his contemporaries, was experimenting with the film camera in a wide variety of

R. W. Paul, another pioneer film-maker

The historical problem of whether Friese-Greene's work was really significant turns on whether his machines would have worked; to prove this, prototypes should be built and tested. There is also the question of how far others with similar ideas established the vital principle of intermittent movement earlier than he did. For example, there is that famous and mysterious figure called Le Prince, of Leeds in England, who disappeared completely on a train in France in 1890 without leaving a trace. He may have anticipated Friese-Greene's ideas by two or three years. Some of the apparatus and strips of film made by these men can be seen in the cinematograph section of the Science Museum in London, including the little wrinkled strips of paper film, faded now and rather pathetic with age, which were once, we may be sure, the trick films. Smith also used close-ups for dramatic and comic effect before 1900.

Later he began to turn his attention to the development of colour; in 1906, he took out a patent for Britain's first famous colour process, which he called Kinema-color. In 1908, Charles Urban put Kinemacolor on the market through the Natural Colour Kinematograph Company. Kinemacolor was a process combining two colours—red and green. Many film programmes, news, travel, documentary and feature, made use of it before the company was forced into liquidation in 1914, after a long series of lawsuits turning on the nature of the patent monopoly for the Kinemacolor process.

Lumière's combined cine-camera, printer and projector—the cinematography. *In 1896, Lumière's agent used apparatus like this to show some of the first cine films to be exhibited in England*

The kind of record shot which Lumière took with his camera

Production, 1896-1905

During the first ten years of the British film industry (1896-1905) many companies were founded and many names made, among them the following (with their years of entry into professional film-making indicated)—R. W. Paul (1896), Cecil Hepworth (1896—he published, in 1897, the first handbook of cinematography ever written; it was called *Animated Photography, or the ABC of Cinematography*), James Williamson (1898), William George Barker (1901, founder of the first Ealing Studios, in 1904, and a pioneer of the newsreel), and Charles Urban, an American who made his career in the British film industry.

Another name of importance was that of Joseph Rosenthal, who, by 1900, was

Cecil Hepworth, one of the earliest of the British film-makers

This is the kind of apparatus used in the "Electric Theatre". In this case, the programme consisted of twenty-four short films and lasted less than one hour. The films were made in 1896 and were each forty feet long lasting less than a minute. Among them were two which were coloured by hand

famous as a British news cameraman and widely-travelled film correspondent who had filmed behind the enemy lines in the Boer War.

These were only a few of the inventors, pioneers, showmen and businessmen who, in one way or another, instituted the production and exhibition of films in Britain. Their output was very large. By 1903, Charles Urban's Trading Company was making 250 films a year; the French Gaumont Company was making 100 through their British subsidiary; the Hepworth Company, 100; R. W. Paul, some 50 a year; and the Warwick Trading

'Refined And Pleasing To Ladies'

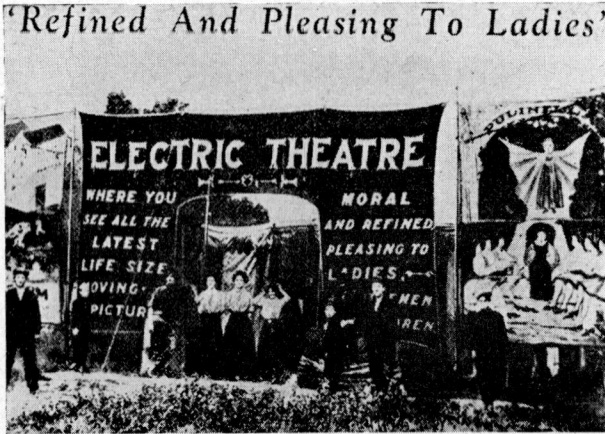

In the early days films were shown as sideshows at fairgrounds

the structure of the industry as we know it today. It was during this period that it moved into its own home—the cinema theatre. Such theatres were virtually unknown in 1906, but, by 1915, there were estimated to be as many as 3,500 in Britain. The cinema had left the fairground and become a centre of family entertainment.

The pioneer producers all built open-air studios. Hepworth began in 1898 with a wooden floor in his back garden, surrounded with movable flats; the scenery was painted in his kitchen. The next phase in studio construction was the glass studio, combining shelter with the maxi-

Company (with whom Charles Urban had originally been associated) was, by 1903, distributing some 500 films each year. The Warwick Trading Company employed a large staff of cameramen abroad, and also handled films made by many of the smaller producers.

Sixpence per Foot

Each main company issued its own catalogues and sold prints of its films outright to exhibitors at home and abroad. The standard price became 6d. per foot. The renting of films did not become customary until comparatively late in Britain, in the decade preceding the First World War. Films were shown in England, as elsewhere, in fairgrounds, music-halls, at local hired halls, and in disused shops. Paul was enterprising enough to have a projector established in the Alhambra music-hall in London; from March 1896 onwards, he gave regular screenings there at each performance. The films of the first ten years ranged from about one minute to about fifteen minutes in length. In fact, it was not until after 1906 that the film industry in Britain gradually began to evolve towards

A typical poster advertising a cinema performance at the turn of the century. The programme, including an example of the newsreel of those days, showing pictures of the contemporary Dreyfus court-martial in France

To-Night! To-Night!

CALDER'S FAMOUS

CINEMATOGRAPH

AND

Popular Concert.

Don't miss seeing the Grand NEW PICTURES of

THE DREYFUS COURT MARTIAL.

The Prince of Wales in Edinburgh.
Sir Redvers Buller Embarking for Transvaal.
Scenes at the Highland Brigade Camp.
The Invercharron Gathering.
The Grand Fire Dance.
Barnum & Bailey's Procession.
The Mysterious Astrologer's Dream.
Spendid Train Scenes.
Grand Coloured Dances.
Comicalities and Burlesque Scenes, &c., &c.

Pictures of absorbing interest and Astounding Transformations.

SPLENDID • CONCERT

By First-Class Artistes.

DOORS OPEN AT 7.30.   CONCERT AT 8 P.M.
Popular Prices—See Bills.

A BRIGHT, UP-TO-DATE, SPARKLING ENTERTAINMENT.

mum amount of sunlight. The most famous of these glass studios was that built by R. W. Paul in 1899; the camera was mounted on wheels placed on permanent rails to allow for rapid positioning, though the camera was, of course, normally kept static during the shot itself.

An Early Feature Film

By 1905, Cecil Hepworth's six-minute

A cine projector made by Pathé Frères in Paris in 1905. The simple mechanism was placed in front of a projection lantern lamphouse and was driven by hand

R. W. Paul's studio, c. 1902

story film of a dog, *Rescued by Rover*, was able to show a considerable flair for the technique of film-making; the story is neatly broken down into scenes, some shot in studio sets and some on location; a sense of tension is built up, and there is a simple visual pattern in the way the story is presented; the audience, too, is identified with the dog when the camera shoots scenes from a low set-up at a dog's eye-level! Film presentation was learning to concentrate, to cut out inessentials, and even, on rare occasions, to use the camera in an unusual way.

The early films contained many scenes of everyday life; they showed streets, landscapes, trains, fire-engines (a wonderful stand-by in programmes!); there were films about country life and even about industry as well as simple nature films. Cecil Hepworth actually made a film about destitute refugees from abroad, living in poverty in London's East End. Then there were the news films (sport, society, Royal occasions); films survive showing Queen Victoria's funeral in 1901 and events of the Boer War of 1899-1902. Travelogues with scenes from distant

Williamson's studio at Brighton. One of the earliest film studios to be built in Britain, it was in use during the first years of the century. Note the glass construction and the track on which the camera is mounted so that it could be moved between shots nearer or farther from the action

lands were always popular. So were vaudeville turns and lightning sketches by cartoonists (often speeded up by the camera!). There were trick films, too, in which cars blew up and then re-assembled themselves; there were custard-pie farces; there were thrillers and melodramas and several lives of Charles Peace, the public's favourite murderer!

Introducing Sound and Colour

Both exhibitors and their audiences felt the need for sound accompaniment to their films, and this was supplied in various tentative ways—the dramatic lecturer and narrator, the pianist accompanying the mood and action with appropriate (and inappropriate) music, and, rather later, attempts to synchronise singing by means of disc recordings played during the film. Laborious systems of hand-colouring added a further attraction to the early programmes; Paul experimented with these as early as 1896. But tinted film stock—blue for night, red for fire, etc.—helped to add drama to the scenes.

These early days of British film-making were characterised by the enthusiasm of pioneers who found that their beloved motion pictures were equally beloved by the public and were a profitable source of income. With all the excitement of schoolboys, they devised a thousand subjects and crowded them (with suitably tempting descriptions) into their film catalogues. They played their full part in building up an industry which, from the very start, delighted the public and proved that these men who had invented the new profession of the film-maker had followed a wise instinct.

1906-1914

The period before the First World War represents the time during which the exhibition of films in Britain became more regularised. Britain was, in fact, late rather than early in establishing cinema theatres—late certainly in comparison with America. But by 1914 there were probably over 4,000 theatres operating in Great Britain.

The programmes offered were one to two hours of films, with the titles changed twice weekly, and often with "live show" interludes from the variety theatre. The popularity of cinema-going increased with each year; an unofficial estimate of the weekly audiences in 1914 was given in the trade Press as seven or eight million. Cinemas, mostly old music-halls adapted for the purpose, were decked in plush and gilt to attract middle-class patrons, and the films themselves varied greatly in their attempt to appeal to audiences which at one end of the scale wanted low comedy and strong drama and at the other the more polite sort of entertainment proper to the middle classes of Edwardian England.

With a gradual change in the nature of the films themselves, the marketing methods also changed. Outright sale of prints of short films was gradually replaced by the system of the exclusive rental of the longer "feature" films, which began to be produced after 1910. Foreign films

For The Texans, *made in 1938, Paramount location crew laid a 2,000-foot track to permit a camera to be used to take tracking shots of stampeding cattle*

In later years the same idea was extended so that the camera was moved during the shot. Now it is a commonplace in the cinema. Here is a camera track built on location in Australia during the filming of a sequence for the documentary, The Back of Beyond

were now flooding the British market, and the agents of foreign producers were already, by 1910, formed into an important branch of the industry.

The general pattern of the film industry was set by 1914. The grouping into production, distribution and exhibition had taken place. Censorship itself began in the form of self-regulation by the industry when the British Board of Film Censors was founded in 1912, following discussions with the Home Office, which wanted to see some form of regulation of films without any establishment of an official State censorship. An independent staff of examinees was appointed by the Board, and the system still operates in a similar manner today.

Other Countries get Ahead

Film-making in Britain, after its magnificent start during the first ten years of production, went into a decline at the very time when production in the United States, France and Italy was developing strongly. To some extent it revived again after 1911, but the war was to intervene too soon to allow a new national movement in production to develop. The whole of the remaining story of the silent film, in fact, both during and after the war, is one of diminished production in Britain. It is curious that the Second World War stimulated British production so remarkably, whereas the First World War almost extinguished it. But the pioneers in British film-making were technicians and inventors, rather than dramatic artists, and their capacities lay more particularly in handling the new medium than in developing screen-plays.

Will Barker and Cecil Hepworth were men whose talents were as different as their natures; Hepworth was modest and retiring, Barker a vociferous showman. Hepworth's style was based on a quiet

Early films were not all crime and adventure. In 1903 Hepworth made a film of Hamlet *with Forbes Robertson, a great stage actor of the period, appearing in the role which we now associate in the cinema with Sir Laurence Olivier*

realism; his work was meticulous from the technical point of view. Barker loved melodrama, sensation and spectacle. Among the films he made at this time were *Henry VIII* (with Sir Herbert Tree, 1911) and a film of Queen Victoria's reign called *Sixty Years a Queen* (1913). Both used established actors of the theatre, and adapted established dramas for the screen. Hepworth formed his own stock company of players, and publicised new actors and actresses, many of whom were to become famous stars in their day.

This was also the period for the spectacular film, popularised by Italy and exploited in England by Barker, with his great armies of extras filmed on location. Stage plays were also filmed, with their casts of players taken to the studio intact from the London theatres where they were appearing.

Sir Laurence Olivier as Hamlet. Like Forbes Robertson in the previous picture he is about to speak Shakespeare's lines "Alas, poor Yorick"

1901. A scene from a newsreel of Queen Victoria's funeral

The Life of Charles Peace (1905) *was the kind of murder-hunt which was produced for the cinema at this time*

At the turn of the century, the climax to a melodrama looked something like this

Americans in Great Britain

If this was not a period of distinction in film production, but merely of effort and output, it was certainly one in which the film industry trained its technicians and established a new profession—that of the film-maker. Alongside the growing number of British technicians there was a tendency, even as early as 1910, for Americans to enter production in Britain. American companies made films in Britain on location with American actors and actresses.

The French companies of Pathé and Eclair also had British subsidiaries. Pathé, however, with the distinguished British producer and director, George Pearson (who before entering film production in 1910 had been the headmaster of a school), established a wholly British unit in London. Nevertheless, British film-making was at that time outclassed by that of Italy, France and America.

Nature, News and Travel

The appearance of the first regular newsreel, in 1910, replaced the older short "interest" films, but travel films remained very popular—particularly the records the cameraman, Cherry Kearton, made of his travels in India, Africa and elsewhere; the film of Shackleton's Antarctic expedition; and Herbert G. Ponting's film made on Captain Scott's expedition to the South Pole. Nature films were always popular, and Percy Smith, one of Britain's finest specialists in this work, began his meticulous work in photomicrography (combining the motion picture with the microscopic lens) as early as 1908. His first famous film, *Birth of a Flower*, was shown in 1910. This showed the movements of flowers in slow motion. Films of bird, animal and insect life fill the catalogues of the period.

Farce and Drama

In the fiction film, the short farces and slapstick comedies of the early period remained in the programmes in forms on the whole less crude than their predecessors. For drama, producers turned to the popular classics of the theatre and the novel, pouring out adaptations with varying technical skill or sensationalism. Actors mimed their way through Shakespeare and nineteenth-century melodrama alike.

Series films (similar, in a way, to the television series of today, and chiefly derived from detective fiction) began after 1911, and historical or costume films were always popular. The technique

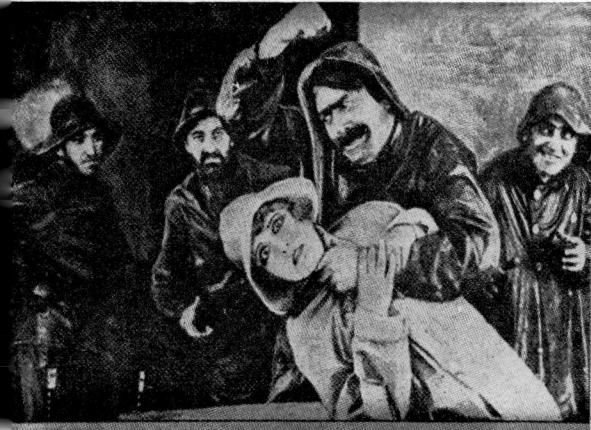

A scene from an episode from the early Pearl White serial, Perils of Pauline. Serials enjoyed a great success from the years just before the First World War to the end of the silent film period

with which all these forms of production were made naturally varied, but without question a high level of professionalism was developed by the better film-makers.

The War Years, 1914–1918

The economic position of the British cinema during the First World War became difficult for a number of reasons,

not the least of which was the imposition of an amusements tax on admission prices. The elaborate cinemas (called now "picture palaces") were expensive to build and to run, yet the admission prices remained conservatively at the old figures, ranging from three-pence to a shilling. Audiences increased during the war and were eventually assessed at some twenty million per week, almost double the figure of today.

The war was filmed and presented not only in the day-to-day newsreels, but in a large number of special "topicals" dealing with particular phases of the fighting photographed by officially accredited cameramen, such as Malin's and McDowell's The Battle of the Somme (1916) or their Battle of Arras (1917). The War Office holds, to this day, a magnificent collection of films giving newsreel coverage of the First World War, often superbly photographed and lacking only sound and a more imaginative approach to make them as living as the records we possess of the Second World War. Without question, the work of the war cameramen was the greatest achievement in British film-making during this period. Animated war maps produced by Kineto were also a popular programme item in the cinemas.

In comedy and drama few films of the war period stand the test of revival. British film-making was dull and conventional compared with the expanding techniques of America. There was nothing in the British cinema to rival the cinematic imagination of Mack Sennett's films, and especially the work of Chaplin.

Sentiment or sentimentality lay behind almost all films made at this time. In general, such films as survive in the National Film Archive cannot be regarded as having any long-term value as works of art. They have "period" value, and they reflect remarkably the middle-class social outlook of the time. As such they will always have value to the student of history and of the film itself.

The acting in these films was mainly overdrawn in keeping with their subjects; nevertheless, acting was perceptibly improving with the employment of established actors and actresses from the theatre and the guidance of more sensitive directors. Set design, structure and lighting moved towards greater realism, and more carefully chosen locations added to the quality of exterior shooting. The camera, however, remained relatively immobile, because to move it during actual shooting was thought to draw attention to it and so destroy the dramatic illusion of the picture. British films were, on the whole, backward, too, in their development of the more inspired form of editing.

The 1920's

George Pearson once called the post-war era of the silent film in Britain "The Twilight Twenties". He had good reason to do so. Production then dropped to its lowest ebb. During a period when America, France, Germany and Russia were making the brilliant films which crowned the concluding period of the silent film, Britain produced a small trickle of pictures from an industry financially depressed almost to the point of extinction.

The growing agitation to save British production led to the generally unsatisfactory first Film Quota Act, which came into force in 1928, and was the origin of the Quota Acts of today. This Act made it obligatory for British exhibitors to show a small proportion of British films in their programmes, starting at five per cent a year and rising by annual stages to twenty per cent. A protective Quota Act, reviewed and renewed every ten years, has been in force ever since; though it has

encouraged the production of many bad British films (particularly during the period 1928-38) it has guaranteed the home industry national exhibition in British cinemas and so has created a basis from which good films could emerge, as well as bad.

The ten years following the First World War saw the production of a few interesting films, and the emergence of several new directors who were soon to become famous—among them Anthony Asquith, Herbert Wilcox, and Alfred Hitchcock. Michael Balcon first appears as a producer in 1922.

The production of factual films in Britain during the 1920's must not be overlooked, although the main movement in British documentary production was first developed after 1930 under the leadership of John Grierson (now famous for his television series, *This Wonderful World*). Bruce Woolfe was the leading producer of factual films during this earlier period. With Percy Smith, he developed the famous nature films, *The Secrets of Nature* (1919-33), which later became *The Secrets of Life*. He also promoted feature documentaries about certain major campaigns during the war, of which the chief examples were *Zeebrugge* (1921) and *The Battle of the Falkland and Coronel Islands* (1928). The link between the film and scientific research was established by Dr. R. G. Canti's study of cancer (1929).

The First Sound Films

1928-9 was the period in which the first sound films from America arrived in Britain. The first British sound film was, fortunately, a good one, Alfred Hitchcock's *Blackmail* (1929), a film which is constantly revived by the film societies today. It was issued in both silent and sound versions; the latter contained very little dialogue, but one vivid and imaginative example of the use of sound.

A girl who has snatched up a knife and killed a man in self-defence goes back home in a state of panic. She tries to sit with the family at breakfast the following morning as if nothing had happened, while a neighbour, full of the news of the murder as it is reported in the papers, keeps repeating the word "knife". On the sound track the word becomes isolated and is repeated and repeated louder and louder until the girl, who has the bread-knife in her hand, drops it with a horrible clatter, while everyone stares at her, wondering what is wrong.

This sequence is of historic importance; it was the first *imaginative* use of sound, and the first sign by Hitchcock of a way of introducing it for shock effect which would be characteristic of him were he to use it today. The sound film was born!

The Feature Film Abroad

Many other countries beside Britain began the production of films at the turn of the century. The principal ones were the United States, France and Italy, but they were soon followed by Denmark, Sweden, Germany and Russia. Italy's main contribution was the development of the spectacle film; it was the vast sets of *Cabiria* that inspired D. W. Griffith, America's greatest director during the first twenty years of film-making, to make his great films, *The Birth of a Nation* (1915) and *Intolerance* (1916).

France had a great artist in the conjurer Georges Méliès, whose fantasies and trick films delighted audiences in every country showing motion pictures from 1896 up to the period of the First World War. France developed, too, the idea of serials played week by week in the cinemas, and Emile Cohl began his strange little cartoons with their match-stick figures in 1908. Max Linder in his one-reel (ten-minute) comedies brought some polish and sophistication to slapstick, and was the model for Charlie Chaplin when he began to make films with Mack Sennett in America after working in knock-about comedy in the music-halls.

The United States

These were the seeds from which the first shoots of the cinema sprang, but the pride of place in the earliest years of the

Griffith's Birth of a Nation *(1915) is now a classic of the cinema. It remains the outstanding example of the early historical spectacular film*

57

Film extras were employed in their thousands and enormous sets were built on the spectacular reconstructions of ancient cities that appeared in films made before the time of Cecil B. de Mille. Cinema-goers were overwhelmed by scenes like these in the Italian film Cabiria (1913) and in Griffiths' Intolerance (1916)

cinema must go to the United States. In spite of cut-throat competition (or perhaps because of it), in spite of patent wars over equipment that eventually made Hollywood the principal centre of production because it was so near the Mexican border, in spite of the sheer gamble and adventure that film-making represented during the first years, America's strange mixture of races due to emigration from Europe produced a remarkable set of men who, in their various ways, combined the diverse temperaments of artists, financiers, show-men and, sometimes, crooks. But many of them developed a flair for making the kind of pictures which delighted popular imagination all over the world. Between them they created an industry ready to supply films in large quantities just as the European film industries were darkened or over-shadowed by the conflagration of war.

This position of being the dominant partner in world film production has never been relinquished by America. By the time the war was over, Mack Sennett was setting the pace with the wonderful

Behind the scenes in Hollywood in the early days. Camera-men are cranking away, the scenario writer has his pencil ready, and the director shows the star how to act the scene

Some stars of the early days:

Above, left: *The romantic hero: Rudolph Valentino in* The Sheik;

Centre, left: *The comedian: Buster Keaton in* The General. *His films are often revived today with great success;*

Below, left: *Charlie Chaplin in* City Lights: *the star who made his own films;*

Above: *Greta Garbo in* Queen Christina: *films were constructed merely to be a vehicle for her extraordinary screen personality*

slapstick comedies in which Charlie Chaplin had been born as a film star in 1914, while D. W. Griffith led the industry in the field of epic and dramatic films. By 1920, Chaplin was beginning his series of feature films with *Shoulder Arms* and *Sunnyside*, working now as writer, actor, director and producer, while Griffith had made his last outstanding film, *Way Down East*. Cecil B. de Mille was already established, starting a career which was to last for forty years. In documentary, Robert Flaherty was finishing *Nanook of the North* up in the Hudson Bay. Hundreds of films were coming in from America, and British cinemas were showing little else but American films in which appeared a host of new stars, such as Mary Pickford, Douglas Fairbanks, Rudolph Valentino and Adolphe Menjou.

Eisenstein's film Battleship Potemkin *(1925), recounting an episode in the early Russian Revolution of 1905, is now a classic. The sequence shot on the Odessa Steps was filmed on location and remains one of the most powerful and moving sequences ever filmed. Once again the use of close-up serves to emphasise action through detail*

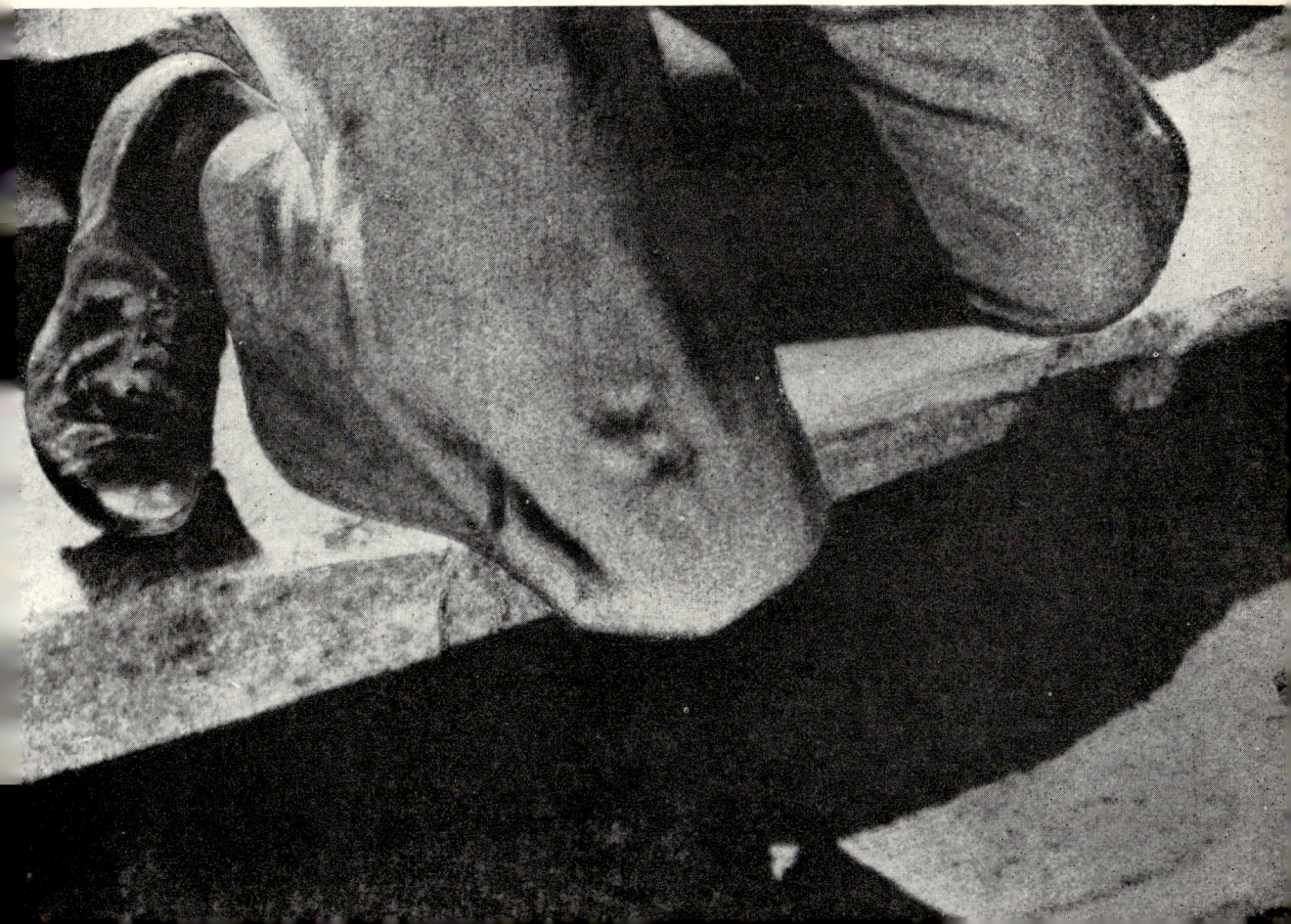

Post-war Developments

After the war, film-making revived in continental Europe. In Russia the most famous directors were Eisenstein, Pudovkin and Dovzhenko, all of them in different ways creating a unique art of the cinema in the service of the communist revolution as they saw it. In Germany remarkable developments were made in studio setting, photography and lighting. In France a whole group of film-makers, either working together or independently, made films which were experiments in conscious reaction against the banalities and conventions of the average commercial film. Among them were some of the leading film directors of the future—René Clair, Marcel Carné and Jean Renoir. The greatest problem in Europe was to stem the tide of American films, which swept in in such numbers that they threatened to extinguish the local industries, especially when many directors and stars began to emigrate to America to try their luck in Hollywood.

There the talent was rich. Star comedians such as Buster Keaton in *The Navigator* and *The General* and Harold Lloyd in *Safety Last* supplemented the genius of Chaplin revealed in such films as *The Gold Rush*. Douglas Fairbanks turned his films of adventure into athletic ballets. De Mille made his first *Ten Commandments* and *The King of Kings*. Fred Niblo made the first spectacular *Ben Hur*. James Cruze started the epic Western with *The Covered Wagon*, and John Ford blazed the trail for the films of the pioneers with *The Iron Horse*. The film of social problems developed with King Vidor's *The Crowd*, and the psychological and realistic film with von Stroheim's *Greed*. It was an astonishing decade, and behind it lay the enormous if precarious wealth of an industry with an audience measured by now in hundreds of millions.

Precarious indeed! For suddenly, after a few public demonstrations of films synchronised with gramophone discs, Warner Brothers launched in October, 1927, *The Jazz Singer*, with lip-synchronised songs and a few words of speech. The industry had to face the recorded music! Sound-on-film was born and the public liked it whether the industry did or not.

History repeats itself in the cinema too: in 1926 the first large-scale version of Ben Hur *appeared. 1930 saw the production of another spectacle—this time a Western—*Cimarron. *New versions of both these films have appeared in the cinema recently*

CHAPTER IV

The Sound Film: 1928—1955

SOUND MADE a great difference to the nature of films. Silent films, beautiful though the best of them were, rarely seemed more than remote shadows, unrelated to real life, unable to speak to their audience except through the clumsy device of printed titles that forced the audience to read instead of watch. As soon as the characters on the screen could talk, their whole being changed from dumb creatures who could only gesticulate to persons as real as ourselves. Through dialogue the action could become much more quick, more complex, more human; the plots of films could become as mature as those of theatre plays.

In the same way, the surroundings in which the action took place—rooms, streets, shops, stations, airports, countryside, sea and open spaces all had their characteristic sounds added to them and became much more real and impressive on the screen. As the technical capacity of films developed, as their photography improved, as colour came to supplement black and white, as sound became clearer and finer in clarity, tone and range, so the image on the screen, combined with its sound track, seemed to portray a world which became more real, more actual with each decade. The sound film was, therefore, a great advance on the silent film, adding a new dimension which brought it very close to real life without losing its flexibility in the hands of the skilful and imaginative film-maker.

The British Feature Film

The first quarter of a century of sound-film production in Britain divides fairly conveniently into three periods—the ten years before the Second World War, the war period itself of five years, and the ten years following the war. Each period differs markedly from the other—alike in its economics and in the employment or waste of the talents at the film industry's disposal. There can be no industry in Great Britain with a less orthodox economy; in film-making the financier and the artist have to learn to work together. No account of the history of the art of the film can disregard the fact that, unlike any other great art, with the exception of architecture, a film cannot come into existence without the patronage of finance and the ultimate support of a distribution and exhibition industry dedicated to business and not to artistic interests. In some periods a liberal atmosphere reigns and the creative talent at the industry's disposal is richly used (for example, during the war period in Great Britain); in other periods (notably in the ten years before the war) talent is wasted or left unused and ephemeral entertainment of the most anaemic kind is turned out at the lowest possible cost.

Not far short of two thousand feature films were made in Britain in the ten years of sound-film production before the war. Yet few of these are remembered today as works of film art. The vast majority of films produced were financed without conscience by British and American interests in order to fulfil the renters' and exhibitors' quota required by the Quota Acts of 1928 and 1938.

However, this generally unhappy period in British film production saw the development of much talent in Britain; many of the best directors, such as David Lean, Thorold Dickinson, Frank Launder, Sidney Gilliat, Michael Powell and Charles Frend were learning the technicalities of film-making, mainly as cutters, writers and assistant directors on films for the most part better forgotten. Also, it must not be overlooked that this was the great formative period for British documentary production, and many creative people preferred to work in the freer atmosphere of documentary than in the uncertain world of the feature film.

The 1930's

With *Blackmail*, Britain entered into a new phase of production. The first stages in the formation of the large-scale film combines followed rapidly as another effect of the Quota Act. The Gaumont-British Picture Corporation was formed in 1927, and soon extended its interests alike over exhibition, distribution and production. By 1929 the Corporation controlled nearly three hundred cinemas. This Corporation also took over, in 1928, the production company previously formed by Michael Balcon, Gainsborough Pictures; Michael Balcon remained as Managing Director. Gainsborough was based on Islington Studios. Another great combine was British International Pictures (later Associated British Picture Corporation) whose interests also developed in all three fields of the film industry.

Balcon and Korda

Michael Balcon's growing success led to him being invited to supervise the new Gaumont-British Studios at Lime Grove, Shepherd's Bush (now one of the BBC's television studios); he undertook this in addition to his duties for Gainsborough at Islington. He became the most prolific producer of major films in Britain, responsible for productions which not only filled his studios, but took units abroad. *Rhodes of Africa* (1935) was made in Africa, *The Great Barrier* (1936) in Canada, *Baroud* (featuring Rex Ingram) in the south of France, *The Constant Nymph* (1933) in Austria, and other British films were made for Balcon in Munich and at the UFA studios in Berlin.

Up to the financial collapse of Gaumont-British in 1936 Balcon's prolific production continued. His most successful films included Hitchcock's famous thrillers, *The*

Rhodes of Africa (*1936*), *a British production made on location*

In 1934 Hitchcock was making thrillers in Britain. This street scene comes from The Man Who Knew Too Much. *It had many of the elements of tension and atmosphere which are associated with Hitchcock's films today. The angle of this particular shot increased the excitement of the action*

Man Who Knew Too Much (1934), *The 39 Steps* (1935), *The Secret Agent* (1936) and *Sabotage* (1936). Balcon also sponsored the American documentary director Robert Flaherty's Irish film, *Man of Aran* (1932-34), and in *OHMS* made a propaganda feature film urging recruitment for the army which forecast in its semidocumentary treatment later films to be made by him at Ealing Studios. John Mills was included in the cast and he gave a good performance; but he failed at this stage to become established as a star.

Parallel with Balcon's work at Islington and Shepherd's Bush, another great producer was beginning his work in Britain— Alexander Korda. After his comparative failure in Europe and America, Korda arrived in England in 1931 and managed to start a new career for himself when he founded his company, London Film Productions, in 1932. In the brief space of four years his success was so great (he made the ever-famous film, *The Private Life of Henry VIII*, in 1933) that he was in a position to build the lavish Denham Studios by 1936. Although British films were by no means unknown abroad, the unique success of *The Private Life of Henry VIII* made Korda world-famous.

E

The brief boom period of investment in production reached its climax—money was poured into production without, for the most part, any regard for the merit of what was made. The ultimate desire of the British producers—the desire to obtain as widespread a distribution for their films in America as American films obtain in Britain—was revived with full force. It was to prove illusory; the American market remains to this day the most difficult of all to enter on a large scale. Korda, however, started on a series of finely mounted productions from London Films (which were some twenty-five years later to be recorded on television)—including *The Private Life of Don Juan* (1934, with Douglas Fairbanks), H. G. Wells's *Things to Come* (1934), *The Scarlet Pimpernel* (1935, with Leslie Howard), *Rembrandt* (1936, with Charles Laughton), *Fire Over England* (1937, with Laurence Olivier and Vivien Leigh). Korda's films were always superbly designed; his brother, Vincent Korda, frequently took responsibility for the *décor*. The third brother, Zoltan, directed a number of London Film productions, including *Sanders of the River* and *The Drum* (1938).

It may seem strange that a company in which the leading figures were mostly Continental Europeans should have so powerful an effect on the revival of the British film. Whereas Balcon came to stand as the strictly *national* producer at Ealing Studios of British films which none the less were to have great international success abroad, Korda aimed always at being an *international* producer based on London. On the strength of this policy, he invited René Clair to London to make the excellent comedy, *The Ghost Goes West* (1935, with Robert Donat). He built up his own stars, such as Charles Laughton, Leslie Howard, Robert Donat, Laurence

Olivier and Vivien Leigh, and developed his own technicians. It was he who appointed Muir Mathieson as Music Director to London Films, and started the fashion for inviting established British composers to write music for films—Arthur Bliss composed a notable score for *Things to Come*. His script-writers included H. G. Wells and even Winston Churchill (who worked on an unrealised script about his ancestor, the Duke of Marlborough). During the 1930's foreign technicians and stars came to Britain in great numbers, many (particularly from Germany and Hungary) to stay and become British citizens; Korda was instrumental in giving many of them employment.

Essentially British Films

The production of films with genuine British subjects and settings started during the 1930's, although it was only to develop fully during the war years to come. These films began to show something of the real British people and, in some cases, a little of the British countryside when the cameras went on location. In 1931 came Anthony Asquith's superb study of the Gallipoli campaign in the First World War, *Tell England*; this was the best war film to be made in Britain until 1940. In the famous sequences of the tragic landings at Gallipoli Asquith used both picture and sound with great imagination.

A very modest film of fisherfolk, *The Turn of the Tide* (1935, directed by Norman Walker) used natural backgrounds and unexaggerated characterisation, and in 1937 Michael Powell directed his first considerable film, *The Edge of the World*, shot on location on the island of Foula in the Hebrides. *Farewell Again* (1937, directed by Tim Whelan) adopted a realistic approach to the study of a variety of British soldiers deprived suddenly of their home leave after three years' foreign service. Carol Reed's first important film was *Bank Holiday* (1938), with Margaret Lockwood, who was by now becoming one of Britain's leading stars; this film was a study of British working-class people on holiday.

Also belonging to this more realistic, native tradition were the films made by John Baxter at Sound City studios at Shepperton from 1933, beginning with *Doss House* (a story of down-and-outs) and *Song of the Plough* (a film of farmers on the Sussex Downs) and leading up to *Love on the Dole* (adapted from a famous book by Walter Greenwood about the effects of unemployment).

Very different from John Baxter, but also in his own way very British, was Herbert Wilcox, who began the sound period with comedies featuring the comedian Sydney Howard, but later made films in which his wife, Anna Neagle, starred, in particular *Nell Gwynn* (1934, with Cedric Hardwicke) and *Victoria the Great* (1937, with Anton Walbrook).

The War Period

British film production could easily have been extinguished by the Second World War. As it was, the quota of British films shown in the cinemas dropped to fifteen per cent. Two-thirds of the studio-space was requisitioned or used for

A scene from Noel Coward's In Which We Serve, *one of the first successful British war films*

other purposes; two-thirds of the technicians were called to the Services or to war-work. But the cinemas and their audiences required the films, and the more serious film-makers (again with Balcon in the lead) set about the production of films many of which took the war itself for their subject. In fact, the first signs that there was to be a national renaissance of film-making seemed to come from these realistic war-films, with their well-written scripts and sharply observed characterisation. Soon these films drove out the melodramas with war backgrounds; the public responded well to the truth, provided there was a living emotion behind its presentation. Realism became box-office.

At the beginning of the period Michael Powell made *49th Parallel* in Canada, with Eric Portman as the Nazi submarine Commander stranded with a few survivors in North America; Asquith made *Freedom Radio* and Pen Tennyson *Convoy*. Then, from 1941, the excellent films came fast:

The Foreman went to France (Charles Frend), *One of Our Aircraft is Missing* (Michael Powell), *Next of Kin* (Thorold Dickinson), *The First of the Few* (Leslie Howard) and *In Which We Serve* (Noel Coward, with David Lean). Harry Watt made a very successful official documentary of the RAF called *Target for Tonight*.

Within the framework of the heroic and patriotic representation of war, these films were realistic. The professional actors in them knew Service life, since most of them were given special permits to appear in films of this nature made in close co-operation with the Services, which rapidly grew conscious of the importance of these films to the morale of both the Serviceman and the civilian. There was, indeed, some rivalry between the Services to get the best films made, with the RAF (after the box-office success of *Target for Tonight*, a film recording a bombing raid over Germany, made in 1941) very conscious of the star-value and screen glamour provided by their fighter-pilots

An effective model shot from San Demetrio, London, *made in 1943*

and bomber-crews. By the middle years of the war a large number of documentaries had been made on every aspect of the war-effort—from the point of view of war industry, agriculture and civil defence as well as the fighting Services themselves. These set the pace for the feature film— and the documentaries themselves invaded the cinemas in full-length form. The Services set up their own film units to make instructional films, and also the occasional full-length film for the cinemas, notably a magnificent series of feature-length films summarising various campaigns in the war: *Desert Victory*, *Tunisian Victory*, *Burma Victory* and *The True Glory* (the latter made together by Garson Kanin and Carol Reed).

War Films at Their Best

It is interesting to compare *San Demetrio, London*, with its cast of actors and mainly studio production, and *Western Approaches*, which was made at sea with a cast of men men serving in the Merchant Navy. In *Western Approaches* the men enact themselves in the reconstruction at sea of a real-life situation where their ship is torpedoed; in *San Demetrio, London*, a group of good professional actors create the script-writer's careful balance of different dramatic characters in the studio reconstruction of a similar real-life situation. Service co-operation with the studios ensured the authenticity of all these films, and such actors as David Niven and John Mills knew exactly how to "place" their

Imagine this scene without the lights, the camera and the structural creations of the set, and here is a realistic shot from San Demetrio, London

Films set in large and spacious territories, such as the Australian "outback" seen in The Overlanders, *have a great attraction for cinema audiences today who mainly live staid lives in cities*

characterisation of the British serving man, his humour, his emotional nervousness, his understatement of the heroic, his quiet charm rather than his passion as the lover.

As the war progressed into its later phases, the war films began to stress character rather than mere action. *The Way Ahead* (Carol Reed), *Journey Together* (John Boulting), *The Way to the Stars* (Anthony Asquith) and *Waterloo Road* (Sidney Gilliat) were all deeply concerned with the effect of the war on the characters of men and women. These films had the same outlook as their predecessors; they formed part of a way of life, a school of film-making generated by the war—the strange mixture of humanity and violence characteristic of the British war film.

Parallel with these films directly concerned with the war, films of normal subjects were being made: *Gaslight* (Thorold Dickinson), *Kipps* (Carol Reed), *Pastor Hall* and *Thunder Rock* (John and Roy Boulting), *The Life and Death of Colonel Blimp* (Michael Powell and Emeric Pressburger), *Fanny by Gaslight* and *Demi-Paradise* (Anthony Asquith), John Baxter's *Love on the Dole*, *This Happy Breed* and *Brief Encounter* (Noel Coward and David Lean), and *Henry V* (Laurence Olivier) were all films made during the war. The accent of all these productions was on quality —whether in the atmosphere and characterisation of a period (*Gaslight, Fanny by Gaslight, Kipps*), the brilliance of presentation in colour and *décor* and acting (*Henry V*), or in sympathy and understanding of character and temperament (*This Happy Breed* and *Brief Encounter*). It was as if the suffering of war gave dignity to both the film-maker and his audience alike, and allowed a range and quality of production that the years of

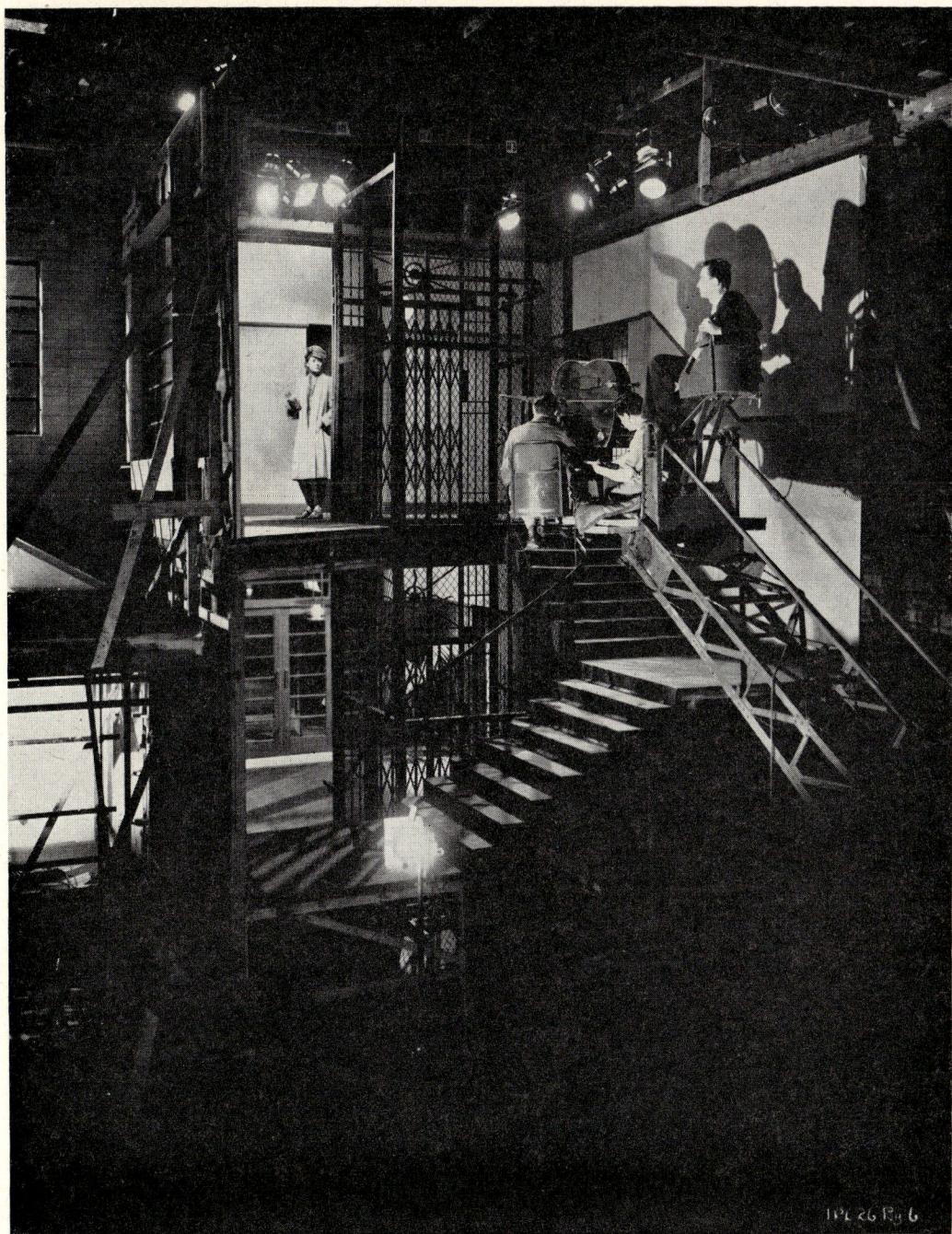

Filming a crane shot in a scene from the Noel Coward-Cineguild production Brief Encounter. *The director is David Lean*

peace seemed unable to sustain with equal concentration.

The Post-war Period (1946-1955)

There was no recognizable trend in post-war British production; the good work was was done almost entirely by established directors, rather than by new, young and urgent film-makers. The reputation of British film-making tended far too much to rest on the achievements of a very few well-known directors (among them Carol Reed, David Lean, Anthony Asquith, Michael Powell and the Ealing group), and to be shaken whenever these few did not make films equal to their best. The normal, so-called box-office film mostly sank to a low ebb of mediocrity due to many causes—among them the restraint on originality imposed by distributors who had too great an influence on independent production and the lack of new writers with exceptional screen-plays to offer. British film-making gives insufficient opportunities to new talent in its constant search for economic security, and production aiming at high quality suffered acutely from the absurdly complex system of finance forced on the independent producer. The rising costs of film-making put an ever-greater emphasis on featuring "safe" stars in "safe" subjects. The average output of feature films remained around seventy a year, and by the mid-1950's several studios were sold for television and other purposes, and this made it unlikely that production would increase substantially in the immediate future.

Nevertheless, many good and even great films were made during the ten post-war years, 1946-55. This is the period which includes Carol Reed's *Odd Man Out*, *The Fallen Idol* and *The Third Man*, David Lean's *Great Expectations*, *Oliver Twist*, *The Sound Barrier* and *Hobson's Choice*, Anthony Asquith's *The Browning Version* and *Carrington, V.C.*, the famous Ealing comedies, such as *Hue and Cry*, *Passport to Pimlico*, *Kind Hearts and Coronets*, *The Lavender Hill Mob*, *Whisky Galore* and *The Ladykillers*, the comedies made by other groups, such as *Genevieve* and *Doctor in the House*, the "location" films—*The Overlanders* (Australia), *Scott of the Antarctic* (Switzerland and Norway), *Cry, the Beloved Country* and *Simba* (Africa); and the films of war and its aftermath—*The Cruel Sea*, *The Divided Heart*, *The Wooden Horse*, *The Colditz Story*, *The Dam Busters*, and *The Small Back Room*; the thrillers—*Brighton Rock* and *Seven Days to Noon*; the "period" films—*The Queen of Spades*; the ballet and opera films of Michael Powell and Emeric Pressburger—*The Red Shoes* and *The Tales of Hoffman*; and Laurence Olivier's *Hamlet* and *Richard III*. Virtually all these films (and the list is representative rather than complete) were the result of the enterprise of independent producing units, some working individually, some through the big producing organisations; only the steady stream of films from Ealing represented a collective style and trend of their own—a quiet realism in their dramas of British life, a quiet humour often bordering on fantasy in their comedies.

Drama and Comedy

With the exception of period films, including those taken from the works of Dickens and Shakespeare, and the films set in the atmosphere of other countries (notably *The Third Man* and *The Divided Heart*), British films after the war found difficulty in solving satisfactorily the difficult problem of revealing the drama hidden beneath the comparatively calm of surface life in Britain. Apart from crime, British life (however "colourful" in certain areas of the great cities) aims at giving the appearance of equability, of avoiding emotional display. The raw edge of passion and of the deeper emotions and instincts (jealousy, pride, passionate love and fear) is naturally present, but conventionally hidden away; to display too much emotion before others is to show lack of self-control or to seem "unbalanced", both qualities of behaviour instinctively disliked by British people of all classes. This can make films in which uncontrollable emotion is shown at certain highly dramatic moments (as in *Brief Encounter* and *The Browning Version*, for example) peculiarly moving, and the war films almost specialised in the "understatement" of emotion, the dramatic tension rising out of the recognition of extreme danger and the nearness of violence and death while behaviour remains conventionally calm and even facetious. One of the reasons why comedy is so frequently successful in British films is that it celebrates the victory of tolerance and individualism over excessive conventionalism and inhumanity, and uses laughter to point the moral of what happens when human behaviour is permitted to go to extremes. This is the essence of the humour behind Ealing Studios' comic fantasies, and the basis of the humour of the strange and solemn gallery of comic eccentrics, fanatics and lunatics with which Alec Guinness has established himself as a star in British films.

While Anthony Asquith and David Lean concentrated on the presentation of dramas and comedies which reveal these particularly British qualities, Carol Reed preferred to create dramatic situations which arise out of differences of temperament between British and other peoples —he used casts of mixed nationality and locations found either abroad or in the less usual places at home, such as London's East End (*A Kid for Two Farthings*), or the special atmosphere of a foreign embassy in a London square (*The Fallen Idol*). Powell and Pressburger were almost ostentatiously non-English in their films of opera and ballet, with results which have been much criticised, but have boldness, colour and flamboyance, when they are successful.

The technical achievement of the best British films (the *décor*, the photography, the sound-recording, the editing) was on a high level—it had the ease of long experience and maturity. British direction and acting at their best had a similar ease and maturity, though few new stars with high acting quality developed immediately after the war; they were to come later. But the chief lack was in the original screen-play itself—almost all the notable films of the period (except for T. E. B. Clarke's Ealing comedies) were skilful adaptations from established books or plays. The detailed characterisation, which is the essence of fine film-making, can only emerge from the finely written, finely observed script. In the end, the cinema, like the theatre and television drama, depends on the writer, the creative dramatist. The post-war period in Britain did not discover its writers in anything like the numbers required to maintain a high level in the *average* film on which the true health of the cinema finally depends.

The Feature Film Abroad

During the first period of the sound film, the principal kinds of film popular with the public remained much the same as those established during the silent period, except for the addition of musicals, which were, at first, mostly adapted from

Westerns have retained their popularity for sixty years—famous examples are Stagecoach *and* Red River

successful stage shows. What happened to the popular film was not a change in kind, but a total change in the way it was produced. There were still Westerns and films set in exotic distant lands; there were still films of war and of crime; there were still historical and "period" films, mostly romantic dramas rather than serious reconstructions of history; comedies still poured from the studios, and so did romantic melodramas, serious dramas, films dealing with varying degrees of responsibility with the more sensational social problems of the period. But all these films, with the addition of dialogue and greater realism of presentation, became stronger, more intense, and gradually more mature and sophisticated. The stars, both actors and actresses, many of whom had been trained in the theatre, could now bring to their acting all the subtlety and the intelligence that had previously been denied them in all but a very few outstanding silent films, in which pose, gesture and expression had been raised to an unusually high level, as in Carl Dreyer's famous film, *The Passion of Joan of Arc*, or René Clair's witty *Italian Straw Hat*, or Pudovkin's tragedy, *Mother*.

All Quiet on the Western Front (*1930*). *This shot shows just how much could be obtained from imaginative studio photography*

Films with National and Geographic Interest

Sound also brought a greatly increased national quality to films. Speech introduced variety of languages to the screen and, as the greater directors and actors took advantage of this, national schools of film-making developed with marked styles of their own. Within the twenty-five years between 1930 and 1955, outstanding films were continuously made in the United States, Russia and France (though French production suffered a considerable eclipse during the war), while the post-war Italian, Swedish and Japanese cinemas produced remarkable work.

The Westerns, of course, were and still are the most typical films of all coming from the United States. Several thousands have been produced since the sound film began, ranging from the historical epic showing the trek west as a great national theme (as in the best films of John Ford) to the simplest cowboy and Indian tussle; nowadays there are even "psychological" Westerns occupied with the problems of violence. The appeal of Westerns to audiences all over the world lies partly in the wonderful settings in such areas as Arizona and Texas, and partly in the pioneer spirit, the struggle for land and livelihood, the establishment of elementary justice in lawless lands. A similar appeal lies in the films that come from countries remote from the experience of audiences in the big cities—the films from Greece and India, for example, or the films of various nationalities that show the backgrounds of the Far East, the Australian continent, Latin America and Africa, or the remote territories of ice or jungle.

War and Crime

There has rarely been a period in the history of the cinema without war films.

In times of peace most countries produce films examining, exposing and discussing the moral problems involved in fighting and killing, as in *All Quiet on the Western Front* (America, 1930) or *Paisa* (Italy, 1946). Some countries, such as Russia and the countries occupied by Germany during the Second World War, made endless films contrasting the suffering of war and occupation with the heroism of resistance. War films are among the most interesting made. In time of war they range from blatant propaganda and displays of courage and prowess in action to the bitterest records of violence and destruction; in times of peace they turn more to the stories of individuals, the experience of war seen from the angle of many kinds of men and women, with courage or without it.

Alongside the films of war developed the films of crime, for crime offers the perennial subject of the forces of law and order ranged against the individuals who prey on society through theft and murder and the exploitation of vice. Every country makes films of crime, but America, which during its rapid growth, has suffered more than older-established countries from the open and defiant practice of crime, has used the powerful techniques of the film to present dramas and melodramas of the criminal in action and of corruption in society. Actors such as Edward G. Robinson became famous in the early 1930's for their portrayal of gangsters, often closely drawn from real-life characters. Many of these films have been criticised because they seem to make a kind of hero out of the gangster—perhaps in any such situation, however disreputable, the few fighting the many may seem as courageous and daring as, for example, the members of the resistance movements were during the war. But in most films the gangster, however thrilling the action he initiates, is shown to be the tyrant, the vicious exploiter and even the weakling and coward that he mostly is in actuality.

A curious off-shoot of the crime film is the film of horror, in which the well-being of society, usually symbolised by beautiful girls, is threatened on a monstrous scale by fiends, giants, madmen, and human beings who turn into every kind of horrific beast. These films were favourites of the German and American cinema even in the period of the silent film, but when sound was introduced every subject of this kind, from Frankenstein to King Kong, the giant gorilla, crept or ravaged its way across the screen; there have, for example, been many famous versions of *Dr. Jekyll and Mr. Hyde*.

History and Romance

For those whose taste is not so much for violence as for romance or the lighter side of entertainment, many kinds of films have been established. The past has been studied and brought to the screen in hundreds of romanticised versions of the lives of historical figures, from Greta Garbo's Queen Christina to the serious but still romanticised Russian portrayals of Peter the Great and Alexander Nevsky as epic figures in national history. The "period" films, whether they are about seemingly real people or fictional characters, give the studio its chance to develop elaborate sets and costumes and to reconstruct the elegance of the manners of the past, or perhaps its horror or degradation, as in the numerous melodramas using the French Revolution for their mostly fictitious backgrounds.

Such films tend to come from countries with a long and picturesque history to exploit; in America, where history in these terms is relatively short, Hollywood has made many expensive, spectacular

Mystery, crime and melodrama continued to flourish in the 1930's. In 1931 Warners made The Public Enemy, *with James Cagney, a film about gangsterdom*

but highly fanciful reconstructions from the history of European countries. But many notable films, such as *Les Enfants du Paradis* from France, *Rashomon* from Japan, *The Red Badge of Courage* from America and the Maxim Gorki films from Russia, have in very different ways created an atmosphere of the past which, whether accurate or not, is strong and imaginative. The past is the most difficult subject of all to bring alive to the screen in any serious dramatic form; most historical films become, therefore, light romantic entertainment or the exploitation of war and violence.

Every nation has its own approach to humour, and each generation has a different conception of what is funny. Humour is to some extent a matter of period, fashion and national temperament. Since films have to be distributed internationally, at any rate by the larger industries, comedy with what is called universal appeal is the ideal, but it is always difficult to produce except in terms of burlesque or knock-about humour. The nations with a marked sense of humour— such as America, which likes crazy humour, Britain, which likes "serious" humour, France, which likes gay or witty

War in the past. The Red Badge of Courage, *a reconstruction of the American Civil War by MGM*

humour, or Italy, which likes every kind of humour, including sentimental humour —have been the most successful in producing comedy. In France, René Clair and Jacques Tati; in America, Frank Capra, Ernst Lubitsch, the Marx Brothers and such stars as Bob Hope and Danny Kaye; they all developed very individual forms of comedy which were enjoyed almost everywhere. With the coming of sound, Charles Chaplin's comedy became increasingly serious and, at times, sentimental; it culminated in his satrical attack on Hitler in *The Great Dictator* and on society as a whole in *Monsieur Verdoux*.

Comedy, Humour and Musicals

Much of America's gaiety and feeling for comedy is expressed through another of her most characteristic entertainments —the musical. Most, but not all, of her musicals originated in the theatre, but from *The Broadway Melody* in 1929 to *Seven Brides for Seven Brothers* in 1954, Hollywood produced musicals that gradually developed the full resources of the cinema in the presentation of singing, dancing and the spectacular combination of picture and music. The best musicals, including the work of Fred Astaire and Ginger Rogers, of Judy Garland, Bing

The dancer, Fred Astaire, in a scene from RKO Radio's musical Top Hat, *one of his most successful films made pre-war. Its expert song-and-dance sequences were simpler than those of the post-war musicals*

Crosby and Gene Kelly (the latter working both as dancer and director), and the directors Vincente Minnelli, Stanley Donen and George Cukor, brought a new art to the screen—the amalgamation of dancing with the technique of the motion picture; this is a new form which might be called cine-ballet.

Human and Social Drama

The fullest expression of the art of the film appears in those films that go deepest into the drama of human experience.

To this, the greatest field of achievement in film production during the first twenty-five years of the sound film, many countries contributed with films that did not in the first place aim to be popular with the international film public. The fact that there are so many films of high quality belonging to this period is a tribute to the rapid maturing of the film, led (apart from Britain) mostly by the directors of America, France, Italy, Sweden, Japan and Russia. In such varied films as, for example, *Le Jour se Lève* or *Orphée* from

France, *The Little Foxes, Citizen Kane* or *Shane* from America, *Bicycle Thieves* from Italy and the Maxim Gorki films from Russia, it was possible to approach very close to both the normal and abnormal experiences of individual people in some form of trouble or difficulty. Some of these examples are typical of good rather than great films, which are naturally rare, but it is the frequency of the good rather than the rare films on which the day-to-day, year-to-year health of the film industry must depend. Other films expanded the individual human problem into the problems of society as a whole—films such as *Kameradschaft* from pre-Hitler Germany, *La Grande Illusion* from France, *The Grapes of Wrath, Dead End, The Naked City* and *Intruder in the Dust* from America, *La Terra Trema* and *Umberto D* from Italy. By any standards, the achievement in twenty-five years was a formidable one.

By the time television was fully established in Britain and North America, and had become a serious rival to the cinema, there could be no question at all that the film had reached very full maturity as an art, and that, however much it had squandered its resources in the over-production of trivial entertainment, it had been able to command an audience throughout the world which was measured in hundreds of millions.

Vittorio de Sica's film Bicycle Thieves *made in Italy, soon after the Second World War, showed similar kinds of social problems with the same realism that* Pather Panchali *was to show later. The effects of bad housing and unemployment are evident in both; but equally, both have a charm and simplicity which is partly due to the revealing use the director made of the faces of his actors both professional and non-professional*

A scene from Pather Panchali, *directed by Satyajit Ray in Bengal in 1955. The simple realism of this Indian film gained an international reputation for its unknown director. Few people in the Western world realise that the Indian film industry is one of the largest in the world today. In spite of this, however, most of India's films are of little interest to audiences elsewhere and are produced solely for distribution in India and certain neighbouring countries*

CHAPTER V

The Documentary and the Short Film

A FILM THAT is called a documentary should, more directly than any other kind of film, present an accurate and understanding portrait of mankind. The way a camera is used depends entirely on the purpose, skill and vision of the man using it. The motion-picture camera is all the more dangerous because it has such a candid air about its living, active portraiture of places and people. It can show only too readily a brilliant surface scene, without any depth or understanding. Only the sympathy of the man employing the camera can bring understanding to what is so clearly depicted on the screen.

Think of a man with a movie-camera seated in the glass dome of a helicopter. Theoretically he can go out to every accessible place on the earth and film it from close quarters. He can observe men and women of every race at work or in leisure. He is the hovering observer—but he never sets foot on their earth, he never enquires what their life means to them. All he has is a record of what they appear to be doing seen through glass.

Reporting and Interpreting

The success of the documentary in the development of human understanding depends at least as much on the man *behind* as well as the man *in front* of the movie-camera. In contrast to the fictional film, it is, of course, primarily the film of fact, the film of interpretation from every level from that of the reporting journalist to that of the deep-seeing poet. It is the use of the roving eye of the movie-camera to capture the most sharply revealing aspects of people in their own environments.

A documentary, like the feature film, must always be understood in terms of the audiences for which it is intended. The manner in which documentaries can reach their audiences is far more flexible than the system of distributing feature films. It is true that some have always been shown in the cinemas, but these have usually to be shaped and presented in such a way that entertainment at least appears to be their chief purpose—for the cinema is a theatre designed wholly for entertainment. Yet much of the best documentary film-making has always been more closely allied to education, and many countries (including Britain in wartime) have adopted special methods of bringing the wealth of documentary, technical and instructional films to the most appropriate places for people to see them—the community social centre, the town hall, the church, the working-man's club, the school, the factory, the technical college, institute and university, or the African compound. And now in men's homes there is developing a vast number of other screens, the domestic television sets, which are ideal for certain kinds of intimate documentary programme, using film as part of its method of production.

A shot from an early documentary: a film recording the Scott Expedition to the South Pole undertaken before the First World War

Education and Publicity

In other words, during the past thirty years or so in various parts of the world a great network of screens has been built up capable of projecting to their audiences a revealing portrait of mankind through motion pictures. In Russia, it began in the early 1920's, when both fictional and documentary films (dramatic reconstruction of phases of the revolution; films celebrating with great enthusiasm the mechanisation of farming, and so on) were dedicated to driving home to literate and illiterate alike the significance of the new communist way of life. In Britain, it began in the early 1930's, when gradually certain departments of the government

and certain progressive industries produced films as part of their public relations—though it took the war and large-scale government finance to establish a nation-wide system of documentary film distribution and exhibition, which took place for the most part outside the cinemas. In Canada, the movement developed in the early 1940's (under John Grierson from Britain), and Canada now has one of the most effective national systems of documentary production, distribution and exhibition (both inside and outside the cinemas, as well as on television) that exists anywhere in the world. In America it has grown up fully in the post-war period; so-called documentary films, good, bad and indifferent, are poured out by the thousand to serve every interest imaginable (commercial, educational, humanitarian), and many of them are available for borrowing, like books, through regional film libraries.

Each country develops its own tradition of production and usage of these films, whether they are produced on a small, carefully considered scale (as in Holland) or in the abundant manner of America, where there are no generally-recognised standards or values in documentary film-making, as there are, for example, in Canada. The two largest annual international displays of this branch of production take place each summer in Venice and Edinburgh. About forty countries submit examples of their documentary films to the Edinburgh Film Festival each year.

The Documentary Film-maker

How much of all this activity on film is valuable? A quality of observation and understanding which in other periods of history might have produced a novelist, a journalist, a dramatist or a poet can now find its outlet in documentary film-making. The post-war expansion of production internationally has obviously outstripped the talent available. Just as a good young journalist needs developing by a good editor who understands the traditional values behind writing for the press, so the documentary film-maker needs development in a tradition which gives him an understanding of the values and responsibilities of his profession. Before he can learn to interpret human life through the camera he must learn what it is valuable to look for in the human scene around him. Almost every documentary film-maker of repute from the days when Robert Flaherty and, subsequently, John Grierson were beginning their pioneer

work has learnt the rule that you must go and live with the people you seek to interpret through film. You may go for a long while (like Robert Flaherty's visits lasting two years or more for each of his major films) or you may go for a few weeks, but length of time is on your side. The values of traditional life in agriculture or industry, in art or craft, in anything worth calling civilisation go deep and cannot be discovered by the stranger (however professionally perceptive) over a week-end.

The professional documentary film-maker must learn (like the journalist and the colonial administrator) how to work both at home and abroad. He will probably achieve initially a reputation for a particular kind of film—such as Paul Rotha achieved for making hard-hitting films designed to challenge the public into thinking about the larger social problems with a national and international significance (*World of Plenty*; *World Without End*) or Basil Wright and the late Humphrey Jennings for making films which reveal a poet's emotional appreciation of the truth behind people and places (*The Immortal Land*; *Fires were Started*). The interpretation through the movie-camera of some detail of the life of one's own country for audiences either at home or abroad is a great responsibility, if only because the general public is always less critical of what is set before them on the screen than they are of the printed word. When, however, the documentary film-maker goes abroad to work, a new responsibility emerges—that of penetrating the foreign barrier to discover the true pulse of life. It is clear that the sympathy he has brought to understanding the people of his own land—nationally and regionally— will assist him in this more demanding task. The response may be a highly personal one—like that of Basil Wright to Ceylon in *Song of Ceylon*. This does not make it less valuable as a study of that people, both for themselves and for the rest of the world. It is desirable in the modern world to encourage the film portraiture of all nations both by their own film-makers and those visiting them from other countries. This is one path towards better international understanding.

Post-war Documentary

Since the war the nature of British documentary production has changed radically. The famous pioneer films of the 1930's with their challenge about social problems (*Housing Problems*; *Enough to Eat*) and their dramatic (and even sometimes poetic) presentation of the facts about industries, agriculture and communications, have virtually no successors today except, in another form, in television documentary. The challenge now is quite different, and is mainly in the direction of developing scientific and technical knowledge. Each year Britain, largely through sponsorship by industry, produces many films on technical and scientific subjects which are sent all over the world. What we lack now are films that increase our understanding of *world* problems, both social and political. This international challenge to our film-makers and other sponsors has still to be met. This is the fault less of the film-makers than of the sponsors. Such films (which would deal with international problems in the same way as we formerly dealt with national ones) can only be sponsored by the UNO, by individual national governments, by wealthy international organisations and by industrial concerns with world-wide interests. These are the films that the best film-makers of our time should be asked to make in far greater numbers—films such as Basil Wright's and Paul Rotha's *World Without End*.

Television Documentaries

World Without End was the first major British-made documentary to have its world première exclusively on British television. There is no doubt that television is an ideal medium for a new kind of documentary presentation (often mixing material pre-recorded on film with the "live" interviews or visits to people and places outside the television studio). Many of the old documentary film subjects (health, housing, education, nutrition, the problems of industry and agriculture, etc.) can now be as effectively handled on television (with its relatively assured audience) as they formerly were on film alone.

Television gives a wonderful opportunity to those who feel that this kind of work is their chosen profession, provided they can discover and develop techniques which will hold the attention of ordinary people in their own homes, and that adequate time is allotted to this kind of work by the various television authorities growing up in different countries. The best documentary programmes have proved they can command audiences measured in millions, and this should encourage the idea of maintaining a proper balance between entertainment and information in the television services.

During the past ten years Britain has become one of the main centres in the world for this tremendously important branch of film production—the documentary films that tend now increasingly to be called "actualities", which perhaps sounds a little more lively than the old term "documentary"!

The BBC maintains a large film studio —the studio, in fact, where the famous Ealing comedies used to be made—and a permanent staff of film-makers who are normally out working all over Britain or, for that matter, all over the world. The principal independent television companies also have their staff of film-makers prepared to find their subjects anywhere they can reach by car or plane. So large has the sheer output of this television film production become that the BBC alone far exceeds each year the total amount of film made by all the British feature companies put together. Many of the films made here for television are increasingly being shown overseas—on television mostly, but also at film festivals and even in cinemas.

Both the BBC and the independent television companies provide through their continuous sponsorship virtually the only opportunity there is for films such as these to be made. Their technique in the end is not remarkably different from that of normal documentaries; they do, however, maintain a close link with "live" television, which takes its subjects as they come with little or no rehearsal, and contrasts with the more extreme forms of careful preparation which go into film productions for the larger screens, which have time and money on their side in the pursuit of perfection.

The television film-maker works faster than his colleagues in standard film production; he is less of a technical perfectionist in what he smooths out or eliminates; he is, in fact, more like a quick-eyed, quick-witted journalist in his assess-

A British documentary of the mid-1930's, Housing Problems, *is an example of the kind of subject which is now being dealt with in television documentary programmes*

The feature-length animated cartoon adapted from George Orwell's Animal Farm *and produced in Britain by Halas and Batchelor:*

(above) *John Halas working at the story-board, producing the original sketches as a guide to the progress of the story*

(left) *Tracing and painting the final drawings on to celluloid transparencies*

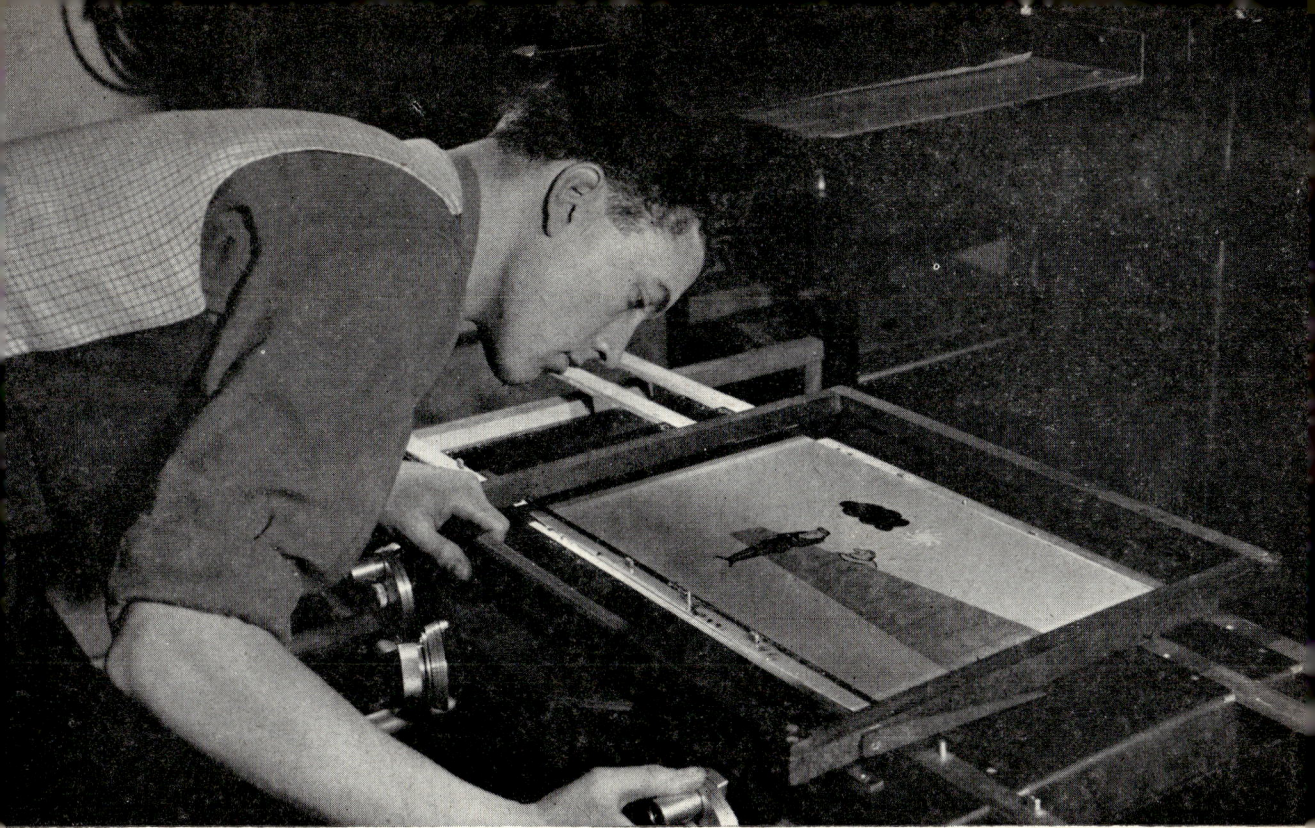

(above) *Photographing the celluloid transparencies containing the moving parts of the picture over the background which remains constant*

(below) *A still from the actual film which was the first British cartoon feature, and was produced in 1954*

ment of the right coverage he needs to bring out the subject in human terms. Both economy and the present size of the screen he serves demand that he use shots that are held longer and concentrate more consistently on faces in close-shot, including people's hesitancies, signs of nervousness and untidiness of action or gesture. But the result of all this new film-making is that we are able to see, face to face, people living every kind of life in our densely populated community as well as people living overseas. In the best of these films we can see them behaving naturally and presented with the respect they should have from the film-makers, without undue hurry and without the smart and spurious air of commercial showmanship that mars far too many actualities of the kind shown in the cinemas.

Cartoon Animation

As soon as the cinematograph was invented it was obvious that the process of making still pictures combine together to produce an illusion of movement could be applied to drawings as well as to photographs. All you had to do was put drawings in front of the camera instead of scenes from real life or the studio. The artist, however, was faced with the problem of devising ways and means of producing an immense number of drawings in series which collectively produced this same illusion of movement once they were photographed and projected on to the screen.

Good cartoon film-making is one of the most elaborate and expensive forms of film production. Each figure that moves in the picture on the screen has normally to be first hand-drawn on paper, then traced on to transparent celluloid sheets and hand-painted, each process repeated twenty-four times for each second of

One of the famous American cartoon characters drawn in the modern style—UPA's Gerald McBoing-Boing

action that you see—all this before the film can be photographed. For each twenty-fourth part of a second a set of these transparent sheets—one for each main character, or group of characters—has to be placed successively on top of the stationary painting of the background. (Similarly, for a puppet film, the characters standing on the miniature set in front of the camera have to be adjusted by hand or by other means the minute fraction of a distance which represents one twenty-fourth part of a second's change in gesture or bodily movement or facial expression.) The task that faces the cartoon animator is to create, on the drawing-board, these minute differences in the movements and expressions of his characters so that the final flow of the motion picture on the screen is both smooth and lively—a formidable, lengthy and expensive process for highly skilled artists. Only comparatively few draughtsmen can develop the combination of wit, dramatic sense, lively technique of drawing and imaginative quality in design and style to do this work well. In addition, a knowledge of music and its dramatic possibilities is essential, because most cartoon and puppet films are very closely synchronised to the special musical scores created for them.

A team has to be built up in the cartoon film studio consisting of key animators, assistant animators, tracers, painters, checkers, all with their assistants and watch-dogs to keep the thousands of drawings true to the original designs, created during the planning stage, as they pass from hand to hand in the long chain of production. A cartoon feature film may well take the best part of two years to make, and will cost as much to produce as a fairly ambitious feature film.

New Methods

More recently, a process has been devised which enables the key animators to work direct on to the celluloid sheets and so cut out the intermediate process of tracing and painting in which the liveliness of the original drawing can only too easily be reduced. This process, which involves using special cell-graph pencils, has been developed in both Britain and America, and gives the artist the chance to draw lines of any quality—thick or thin, strongly or subtly shaded—direct on to the celluloid sheets which will go before the camera. The special coloured pencils

A scene from Skeleton Dance, *one of Walt Disney's earliest cartoons, produced in 1929. This was the first of the "Silly Symphony" series*

Snow White and the Seven Dwarfs *was the first cartoon feature film to be made. When finally produced in 1938 it had taken Walt Disney some three years to make*

produce work that can be either corrected or rubbed out easily, All the complex business of using special inks and paints to trace the animators' work on to the celluloid can thus be avoided, and this has greatly reduced the cost of animation and brought it within the range of the comparatively low budgets available for television programmes, quite apart from its use in the commercials sponsored, i.e. paid for, by the advertisers.

Cartoons are a very special form of film art. The reason for going to all this trouble is quite simply that the cartoon film can perform actions that no other kind of film can present. We like to think that animals can share many of our human characteristics. The cartoon in its earliest developments during the period of the silent film enabled them to do so. Throughout the world the comic adven-

tures of Krazy Kat, Felix the Cat and eventually Mickey Mouse, whom Walt Disney launched just as the sound film arrived, became extraordinarily popular with audiences of all ages.

On television some of the old cartoon characters, such as Popeye the Sailor, are being revived in new forms and joined by original characters, such as Huckleberry Hound from America and Foo Foo from Britain. In puppetry, the paper sculpture characters of Snap, Sniff and Snarl were specially created in Britain for television and are also being shown in many parts of the world. Animals or humans, these creatures of fantasy could only come into existence through the technical and artistic combination of the two worlds of the graphic artist or the puppet-maker on the one hand and the film-maker on the other.

The Grand Concert *is one of the Snip and Snap paper sculpture series produced for ABC Television by Halas and Batchelor. The principal characters are all dogs*

Foo-Foo is a character who has appeared in a British television cartoon series drawn in a style reminiscent of the early cinema cartoons and is another brain-child of Halas and Batchelor

Nor is cartoon animation confined to this kind of comic fantasy. Many episodes in Walt Disney's exciting and often sensational series of feature-length cartoons are far more dramatic, melodramatic or even horrific than they are funny, while the first wholly serious cartoon feature, *Animal Farm*, was produced in Britain as an adaptation from George Orwell's famous political novel about dictatorship presented in the form of a modern satirical fable in which the characters were all animals.

Animation (cartoons, puppet films, films that make objects, models and diagrams move) is used now for most purposes: advertising, instruction, scientific and technical films as well as entertainment. In Disney's film, *Man in Space*, science and entertainment were combined and animation was used to explain in the cinema programme a difficult technical subject in which everyone is interested. Animation is a unique branch of film-making; its range and use will increase as more people realise the greater opportunities it offers to the artist, the film-maker and the public, not only in entertainment, but

A scene from Concerto for a Sub-machine-gun, *a Jugoslav cartoon, shows the influence of UPA*

in helping to make our complicated modern world clearer both to the student and the ordinary member of the public.

The Experimental Film

All the arts, including the film, have their advance-guard—the artists who for many different reasons (a strong reaction against tradition, a need to discover new techniques or new forms to express new attitudes, or quite simply to shock convention out of its complacency) produce work outside the normal that expands the strength and vision of the medium. Every art and every society needs a constant injection of new ways of observing and thinking; the fact that a great deal of rubbish is produced at the same time under the cover of new art does not matter, provided the critics are sharp-eyed enough to see that the rubbish does not steal all the public attention.

In British film-making this advance-guard has existed both inside and outside normal professional production. For example, when Percy Smith, as early as 1908, began his experiments in photographing with varied motion the activity of Nature seen under the microscope, he began as an amateur who was later to become a professional. So, much later, did Dr. Richard Massingham with films that introduced his particular kind of crazy humour. A few years ago Peter Foldes, who made (together with his wife, Joan) the brief but striking cartoon film, *A Short Vision*, on the destruction of life by a nuclear bomb, is a painter who works only now and then as a film-maker. On the other hand, Lindsay Anderson, who was one of the pioneers of British *avant-garde* production in the so-called free

cinema movement of the 1950's, was and still is a professional film-maker who has directed films of many different kinds (including some of the *Robin Hood* series

Man in Space; *the cartoon technique is very useful for scientific, documentary and educational subjects*

for television), but who turns to fully creative film-making when the opportunity comes his way or when (as in the case of his satire on a fun-fair, *O Dreamland*) he is able to get enough money together to make it for himself. The film-maker with a highly individual vision is a fortunate man if, like the late Humphrey Jennings, or like Norman McLaren in Canada, he finds continuous sponsorship as a professional artist for his own particular style of work.

Sponsorship

Films costing what they do to produce on the professional level, sponsorship becomes a matter of great importance to the more experimental film-maker. The famous *avant-garde* movement in France, the conscious creation of a group of young artists in the silent film who built up their own lively audience, to a large extent disintegrated when the sound film became fully established, with its greatly increased costs. In Britain, one of the most striking characteristics of the pre-war and wartime documentary movement was that a strong nucleus of professional film-makers, working within both State and industrial sponsorship, were able to experiment boldly with their medium in such films as *Drifters* (Grierson), *Song of Ceylon* (Wright), *Shipyard* and *World of Plenty* (Rotha), *Housing Problems* (Elton and Anstey), *Coalface* (Cavalcanti), *Night Mail* (Watt and Wright), the work of Jennings, of Len Lye (in such films as *True Tattoo*, anticipating the later experiments of Norman McLaren), the accomplished technical films evolved by the Shell Film Unit, and the wide range of animated cartoon films sponsored by the government in the public service and made by Halas and Batchelor.

Since the war it has become much more difficult to find outlets for experiment with the recession of this particular kind of broad-minded sponsorship (with notable exceptions, such as the oil industry). Artistic experiment, as distinct from purely technical experiment, can only be spasmodic, when a subject and a sponsor happen to be brought together at the right time and place with the right film-maker. An only too rare example of this occurred when the Ford Motor Company gave Karel Reisz, Lindsay Anderson and their colleagues a free hand to produce *Every Day Except Christmas*, their portrait of the night-workers in London's fruit and vegetable market in Covent Garden.

Sponsorship which permits experiment today in Britain has, therefore, no particular pattern. It may occur within television, and result in the brilliant films on art and artists made by John Read on the work of Henry Moore, Graham Sutherland, and L. S. Lowry, or Denis Mitchell's sad, sharp film on life in prison made in Springfield Gaol, Manchester. It may happen within normal commercial sponsorship, especially in the case of technical subjects or public relations, such as the animated film, *Earth is a Battlefield* (sponsored by the Iron and Steel Federation) or *For Better, for Worse* (a satire on television sponsored by Philips of Holland). It may arise out of some special occasion, like the 1951 Festival of Britain, which saw the sponsorship of abstract films in the third dimension made in Canada by Norman McLaren, or Basil Wright's and Adrian de Potier's *Drawings of Leonardo da Vinci*, which was paid for by money raised from a number of sources by a special committee. Nor must we overlook the purely amateur film-maker; although his resources (both financial and technical) are strictly limited, he is at least completely free to make whatever he wants.

Momma Don't Allow *was a film made early in their careers by Karel Reisz and Tony Richardson at a London dance club. Both of these directors now make feature films*

Scientific films often use photo-micrography which links the microscope to the movie camera. Minute animals, a fraction of a millimetre long, from the Shell film Unseen Enemies

The British film industry itself sponsored an Experimental Film Fund during the 1950's, with a grant-in-aid of £12,000 to be administered by the British Film Institute, which set up a committee of film-makers under the chairmanship of Sir Michael Balcon to select the subjects to be subsidised or assisted. These have included *A Short Vision, Figures in a Landscape* (a study of the sculpture of Barbara Hepworth against the Cornish scene where it is produced) and *A Door in the Wall*, a short film based on a story by H. G. Wells and designed to give a technical demonstration of the dynamic frame, a system using variable picture dimension on the standard screen to emphasise the dramatic needs of the action.

However the costs of its films are met, from private sources or through some form of sponsorship, experimental cinema refuses to compromise with the staler values of the box-office. It wants to use the camera and microphone with the same freedom of style as the painter uses brush and canvas to portray the subjects of the visible world—with the realism of the candid camera (*Nice Time*), with satire (*O Dreamland*) or with poetry (*Every Day Except Christmas*). Free cinema carries with it the true spirit of the *avant-garde*, and, like the movement in the French cinema thirty or so years ago, has already succeeded in bringing a new generation of artists, such as Karel Reisz, director of *Saturday Night and Sunday Morning*, into the full-scale professional cinema.

Children's Films

One of the most interesting developments of the film industry in the last twenty years has been the special entertainment films for children—that is, for boys and girls of from roughly six to twelve years old. No one knows who really made the first children's entertainment film, but, in the late 1930's, the Russians began to produce an occasional feature-length fairy story and some beautiful short coloured cartoons. However, there was no definite long-term plan of production for such films. The first country to treat children's entertainment films as a serious part of the film industry was Great Britain.

In 1944, although bombs were still falling on London, J. Arthur (now Lord) Rank, considered very seriously the type of films shown in the Children's Cinema Clubs that were organised in the cinemas belonging to his organisation. When he was told that the most harmless adult films were selected, but that there were no story films really intended for the pleasure of boys and girls, he decided to make some. He set up Children's Entertainment Films (CEF) within the Rank Organisation. This group produced every kind of film, from cartoons to features, with cinema club audiences in mind. Above all, CEF revived the serials, and children flocked to the clubs from week to week to see the next thrilling instalment. These films were very well produced and in no way inferior to adult films but the stories, the actors and the production were particularly suited to younger film-goers, although older ones loved them too. The films were produced all over the world as soon as peacetime conditions prevailed again, and some of the CEF films, such as *Bush Christmas*, made in Australia, have become international classics. In 1950, the Rank Organisation could no longer continue to finance CEF. The whole British film industry took on the job because producers, distributors and exhibitors had come to believe that children's entertainment films were an essential part of national film life. As the Children's Film Foundation, paid for

Song of the Prairie is a charming puppet film, one of the many made in Czechoslovakia which is a centre for this kind of film production

by the industry, the new-style CEF continues to produce first-class children's films of all kinds. Other countries have not been slow to follow this example, and Russia, Czechoslovakia, Poland, Bulgaria, Germany, Italy, India, the Chinese Republic and the Scandinavian countries are all producers of children's entertainment films, as well as Australia and, in a small way, Canada. However, all countries do not always agree on what really constitutes such films and some are too full of instruction, or of morals, to be really international in their appeal. Many, however, are outstanding, especially the Czech puppet films of feature length and the Russian coloured adventure features, but only the Children's Film Foundation produces popular serials for boys and girls.

CHAPTER VI

How Television Works

THERE ARE various ways by which a pattern or a picture can be explained to someone else so that they can reproduce it. A knitting pattern may be written down, K.2, P.1, meaning: knit 2, purl 1. Pictures can be bought with numbered squares marked over them and a chart which explains what colours to put on what numbers to get the right colouring. Patterns in mosaic—little squares of marble or coloured stone—can be written down—6 white, 2 blue, 9 red—and pictures of objects can be accurately reproduced in this way.

By filling in squares or dots on a piece of paper with dark or light shading, you can copy a picture from a paper which was planned before. In every case the picture or pattern is there; it is broken up into the different colours or shades that make it up, it is communicated in some way and then it is reassembled elsewhere.

Transmitting and Receiving

So it is with television. The picture which is to be televised can be any scene, indoors or out. It is broken up by the television camera into dots arranged in lines. Some of these dots are dark and some are lighter or even white. This pattern, which has been dissected by the camera, is transmitted in the form of wireless waves. The pattern carried by the waves is received by your television receiver and is reconstructed on your television screen. The pictures you re-ceive come very quickly, at the rate of 25 per second. As in the case of films, the continuity of vision by which the impression made by each picture remains in your mind makes you feel that you are seeing not a sequence of pictures, but one moving scene.

There are four operations involved in television: dissection and transmission, which are the affair of the television companies, and reception and reconstruction, which take place in your home. It is up to you to see that your aerial and your set work as well and efficiently as does all the complicated machinery of the television producers.

To reproduce a picture, a television camera breaks it up into lines made up of dots. It uses a light to "scan" the picture and records electrically whether the spot it is "scanning" is dark or light. The scanner starts at the top left-hand corner of the picture, and zigzags down from top to bottom. It covers the picture 25 times per second, making 405 zigzags. The number of lines into which the picture is divided is important. If there were only about twenty lines, the reproduction of the picture would be very rough-and-ready, with no delicate variations of light and shade. In Britain each picture is divided into 405 lines, but in the USA and Europe television companies use 625 lines. The accuracy of the picture reproduction is called definition.

The scientific discoveries of the nine-

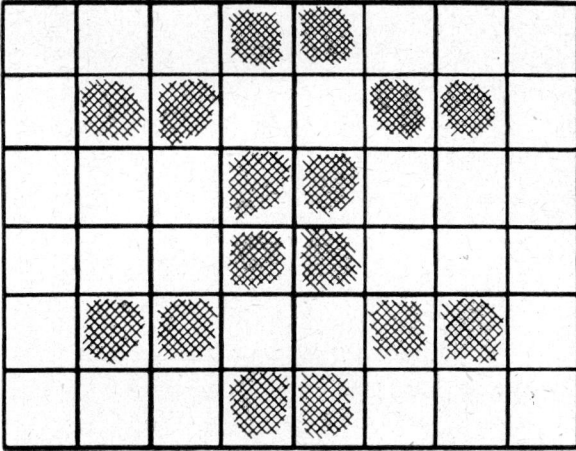

This is the beginning of the formation of a picture on the screen of a television camera. All pictures in black and white consist merely of irregular areas of light and shade and the drawing suggests that the spot which is illuminating each square in turn meets something which causes it to light up some squares with less intensity than others. When the movement of the spot of light is very rapid, the screen appears to be illuminated by a steady picture, in spite of the fact that each spot is lighted in turn

teenth and twentieth centuries, electricity, photography, wireless and electronics, have all combined to give us television. The history of television is short, as far as scientific discoveries go, and is the result of the work and research of many men in many countries.

If an arbitrary starting-point for this development is to be chosen, and we must start somewhere, the choice would fall on an event in Sweden in 1816. In that year a chemist, J. J. Berzelius, discovered a new element which he called selenium (Se). An element, by the way, is a substance which is complete in itself and not the result of two or more substances joining together, like water, which is a combination of hydrogen and oxygen (H_2O).

An Unusual Element

It was fifty years later that an English engineer, called Willoughby Smith, was employed in laying an electric telegraph cable across the Atlantic. He wanted to be able to communicate with the shore while he was on the cable ship, and for his apparatus he needed to find a material which would not easily be affected by electricity. Someone suggested selenium,

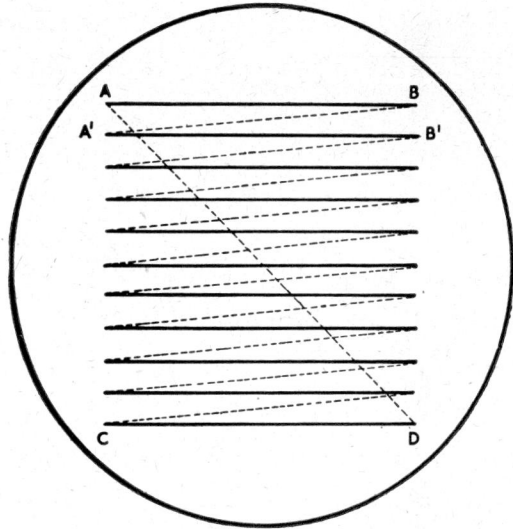

When the beam of electrons in the cathode ray tube is moved rapidly over the screen it obviously takes a certain time to move back from the end of one line to the beginning of the next. Such movement is of no use for scanning purposes, and is consequently arranged to take place as rapidly as possible. Some idea of the speed of the movement can be gained from the fact that it takes no more than one twenty-fifth of a second to scan the whole picture. In this drawing the backward movements of the spot of light are shown by dotted lines. Starting at A, it would move to B, then return to A^1 on the line below. Arriving at the bottom, D, it would flash back instantly to A, and the whole process would begin again

This is not a puzzle picture but an actual representation, many times enlarged, of the way in which a picture can be built up on the television screen by a series of dots, the dots being illuminated by greater or lesser degrees of light. On the actual screen, of course, the dots would have varying weights of tone, they would not all be of the same strength of blackness; but even with this simplified drawing a surprising effect can be obtained by viewing the picture at a distance of about fifteen feet. Try it, by standing the book up on the table and walking back from it. Suddenly, the squares will turn into a picture for you

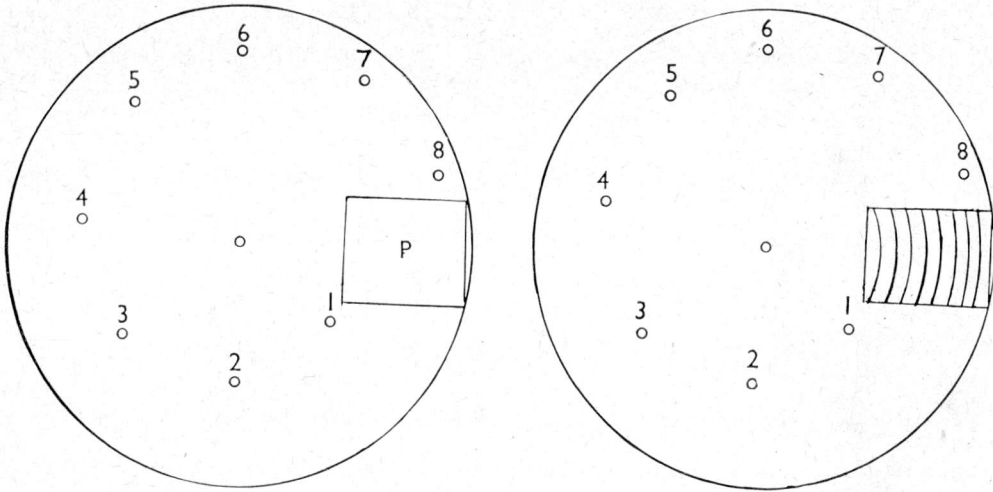

Nipkow's disc—a crude scanning device. The device consists of a rotating shutter (left) pierced with small holes set spirally. The rectangle P represents the picture to be scanned. When the disc is rotated (right) each hole in turn will sweep across the picture along the paths shown above

but added that it was unreliable. Sometimes it resisted electricity; sometimes it appeared to be influenced by it. Willoughby Smith found that selenium resisted electricity in the dark, but transmitted it in the light; selenium was "sensitive" to light and was described as "photo-electric". Willoughby Smith realised at once that selenium could be used for transmitting pictures—electrically. They were still pictures, of course. There were no moving pictures yet.

In theory, it should not be difficult to divide a picture into lines made up of little squares, to put a piece of selenium opposite each square—divided from the picture by a lens to focus—to connect each piece to a battery and get varying electrical impulses from each piece of selenium, strong or weak, according to whether the square opposite it is light or dark. These impulses could affect carefully prepared and connected apparatus, either strongly or weakly, so that the picture is reproduced by the varying strength of the impulses.

But this theory, which sounds simple, was immensely difficult to put into practice. There were no electric lamps until 1878, so the first experiments were made by the impulses affecting a pencil which pressed hard or softly.

Two years after the electric lamp was discovered, a Frenchman, Senlacq, suggested that the impulses from the pieces of selenium should be connected with the lamps and the pattern of light and shade they made, i.e. the picture, thrown on to a screen.

Nipkow's Disc

But this method was far too slow and cumbersome to be practical. Television had to wait for the next research worker, this time a Russian working in the USA, called Nipkow. He patented an electric telescope which is usually called "Nipkow's disc". It was a disc which turned rapidly in front of a picture and which was pierced with holes arranged round it in a spiral. The picture which the wheel scanned was divided into as many lines as there were holes in the disc. The holes passed one by one over the picture, going left, and the scanning was not horizontal, but vertical. If selenium were placed before the place where the hole was at the bottom of the wheel and the selenium were then attached to a battery and a lamp, light impulses of varying intensity could be transmitted through a prism on to a similar disc and the picture would appear in front of the bottom hole. One difficulty for Nipkow was to make certain that the two discs turned at exactly the same pace, but the major problem was that the scanning was too slow for any persistence of vision, i.e. to create moving pictures.

The Cathode Ray

Then came another development that was to help in the evolution of television— the cathode ray. It had long been known that if wires carrying electric current at high pressure are brought near to each other, the electricity leaps across from one to the other and, as it does so, makes the air in the gap so hot that we see a spark. The electric lamp, discovered by Swan in 1878, worked on the principle that if there were no air in an electric bulb, the wires in it would get white hot, but could not spark. In the same year, 1878, another scientist, Crooke, tried the experiment of fixing two metal plates, negative and positive, in a glass bulb with the air withdrawn and at a distance apart. After varying reactions, a glow appeared round the negative plate, called the cathode, and a glow appeared also on the glass at the end of the tube in front of it. This glow came from an invisible ray—the cathode ray.

Further work and experiment led, after nine years, to the production by Braun in Germany of a cathode-ray tube. Braun found that, by using a magnet, he could move the ray about on the end of the tube, which acted as a sort of screen. This was the beginning of the modern tube in a television set and was first used in this way in 1907. The ray scans the picture, which then appears on the screen at the other end of the tube.

So much for the television picture. But what about the sound? All over the world, scientists were working to develop

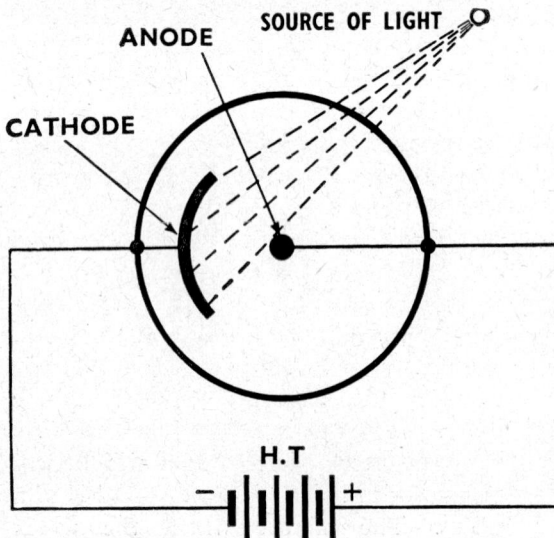

The action of the photocell. The anode is connected to the positive pole of a high-tension battery and the cathode to the negative pole. There is thus a high positive charge on the anode and this gives it a powerful attractive force for any electrons which may be released from the cathode. This does not happen, however, until the light falls on it, the cathode being made of material which is sensitive to light instead of to heat, as in an ordinary valve

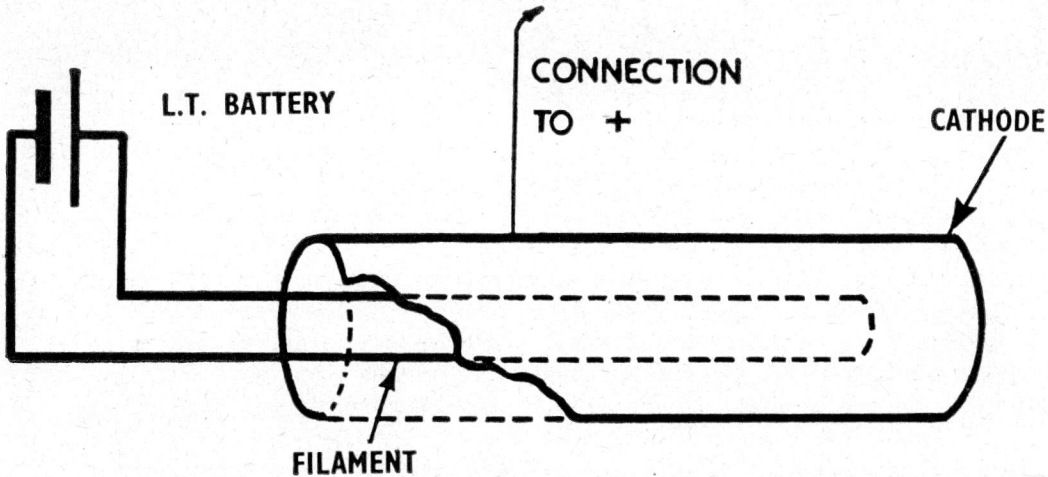

The indirectly heated cathode of the cathode ray tube—it is possible to make the filament behave as the cathode but it is preferable to have the two separate, so that the cathode, shown here as a tubular cover over the filament, is independent of the heating current. This makes for a much steadier flow of electrons

communication by sound, just as they were working at communication by picture. First they made it possible to send messages by electricity along wires, and indeed by cable; such messages could be sent by Morse across the Atlantic. But wires and cables were difficult to handle. Scientists concentrated on how to communicate without them—communication that would be "wireless".

Sound without Wires

In 1896, a young Italian called Marconi arrived in Britain, where he hoped to get more support for his ideas and schemes than he had achieved in his native land. Nor was he disappointed. With British encouragement, financial and scientific, he perfected a way of sending messages without wires. First his messages went from one room to another. Then, in 1897, he successfully sent his wireless signals across the Bristol Channel, next across the English Channel and, in 1901, across the Atlantic. The immense speed with which wireless telegraphy, which

used the Morse system, was able to develop was due to the many scientific experiments and the enormous amount of research going on all over the world. It was as though the pursuit of knowledge were a kettle of water which was almost cold at the time of Roger Bacon (the thirteenth-century Franciscan friar who first emphasised the importance of practical experiments), beginning to simmer in the age of Newton and was now boiling furiously.

From Lamps to Valves

Men could communicate by wireless, but now they must find how to transmit the human voice. By 1881 the telephone had been developed so that the human voice could travel over wires. Three years earlier, the microphone had been invented so that the human voice could be recorded. As before in this story of the development of television, there was a pause while men waited for the discovery that would enable them to press on. This discovery came when Sir Ambrose Fleming, an old colleague of Marconi's, developed Swan's electric lamp. In 1904 he had suspended a small metal plate above the filament in the lamp and found that a strong electric current would cross the space between. Fleming used this altered lamp—called a valve—to strengthen weak electric impulses so that wireless messages could go farther. Two years later an American, Lee De Forest, improved Fleming's invention so that the valve would actually magnify electric currents and the sounds they produced. This lead eventually to what is called today an amplifier, both for sending and receiving wireless messages.

The First World War, 1914-18, led to great activity in the field of wireless telegraphy, for both sides in the conflict needed it for communication. Before the war, De Forest had been able to transmit music from a gramophone record for a few miles, but, after the war, the world was ready for entertainment and instruction by wireless as we know it today. In 1921, the BBC was set up by Charter in Britain—one year after radio had started in the USA. With the establishment of national wireless or radio, television came one step nearer.

Shelford Bidwell

As early as 1908 an English scientist, Shelford Bidwell, had written on the subject of television to the scientific magazine, *Nature*. Bidwell had a scheme for sending moving pictures by wireless,

This is how the lens of the television camera focuses the image of an object on the screen inside it, and how the electron gun and its beam of electrons then "scans" this light image and transforms it into a series of radio-pulses for transmission

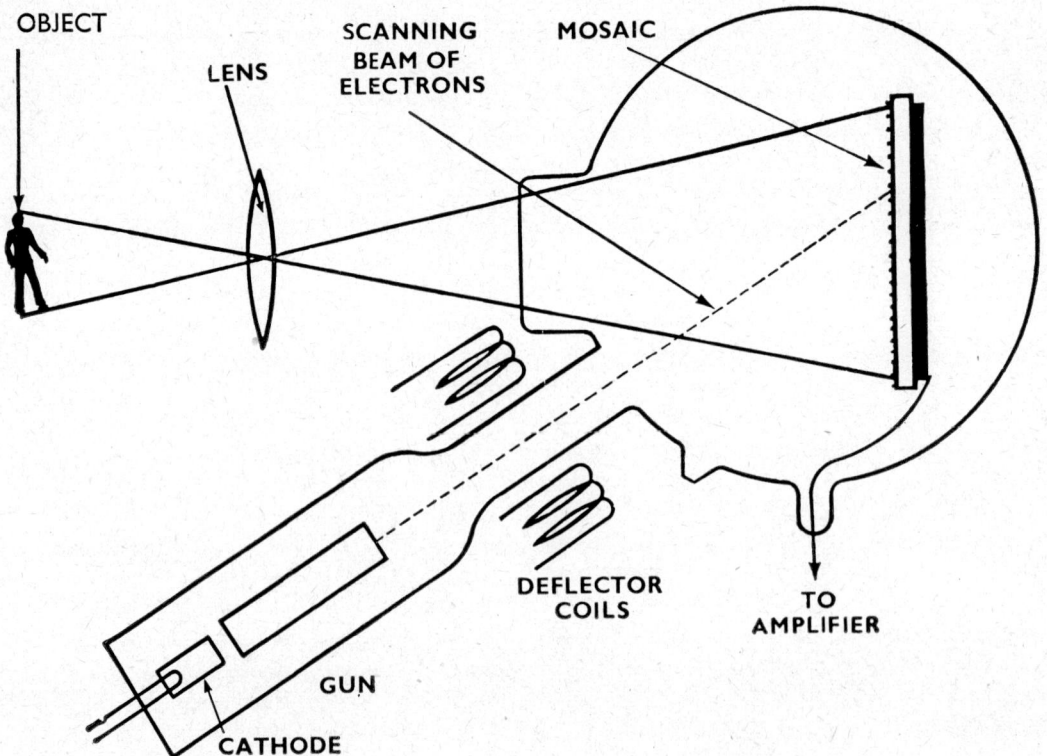

but, unfortunately, his transmitter could not scan quickly enough. This was the real problem—how to scan. Television was available in theory, but not in practice.

Since Bidwell's plans were obviously so complicated that they would never be really practical, various other scientists felt that he was working along the wrong lines. Among these was one of Marconi's early supporters—Campbell Swinton. He too wrote to *Nature*, the magazine in which scientists of all kinds air their views and suggest possibilities for further scientific development. Swinton said in his letter that television could possibly be achieved by using cathode-ray tubes both to scan the picture and to receive it. But apparently nobody paid any attention to this letter, even though he followed it up by working out his ideas in detail and explaining them, in 1908, to a scientific society. Like many thinkers, he was before his time. In 1914, the First World War broke out and, when it ended in 1918, the scientific world was concentrating on radio, not television.

The story of how television became a practical proposition and how it developed in Great Britain is so closely associated with the career of one man that it is most easily followed in the life of John Logie Baird.

CHAPTER VII

John Logie Baird

*T*he *Oxford Dictionary of Current English* defines a martyr as "one who undergoes death or suffering for any great cause". The history of science contains the stories of many martyrs, men and women who have sacrificed health, wealth, family, even life itself to the furtherance of knowledge. One of the authors of this book was the first person ever to have a film made by X-rays of the bone movements of her arm. The rays were not sufficiently strong to harm her, but the man who made the film died only a few years later from the effects of the rays with which he was experimenting. A mere thirty years after that event, we expect today to have a broken bone X-rayed as a matter of course and no one suggests there is any danger now, so short a time after a martyr gave up his life.

One of the greatest martyrdoms that a scientific worker can suffer is to have his work unappreciated or, worse still, to have another research worker in the same field complete the job and announce the results a few weeks before his labour of years is ready to be announced. One man who suffered in this way was John Logie Baird.

Amateur Photography

Baird was born in Scotland at Helensburgh, near Glasgow, in 1888. His father was a minister in the town and his family had a high record for education. But John was too delicate to go to any of the famous Scottish public schools, which sixty years ago practised a high degree of austerity. After some years at a preparatory school, he went on to a private school which, like most schools of the period, taught very little mathematics and no science. Even at this private school John suffered from an almost perpetual cold which prevented him from playing any games. But he was determined to follow some pursuit and took up photography as a hobby. By saving every halfpenny he was given, he was able to buy a good camera. A good camera will not take outstanding pictures by itself, but John used his so skilfully that he became Chairman of the school photographic society. Probably he enjoyed the discussions on the theory and technique of photography as much as or more than he enjoyed the practice of his skill.

Even at school the desire to invent was very strong in John. He and some friends were fired by the stories of the Wright brothers, who were succeeding in building and demonstrating flying machines in the USA. Accordingly, they too designed a glider into which they intended eventually to put an engine. When it was built, it was rather like a kite. They got it on to the roof of the school, John climbed into it and it was launched. Unfortunately, the glider broke in half and the intending airman landed ignominiously on the school lawn. Luckily, he did not hurt himself, but his desire to invent appears to have been temporarily checked.

From school he went on to the Royal

Technical College in Glasgow. Here he achieved a diploma in engineering which gained him entrance to Glasgow University. He took his B.Sc. and got a job with an electrical supply company. But his weak health broke down under the work. He had to resign this job and several others which he tried. Thinking that a warm climate might suit him better, he went to the West Indies, but here he could find no one who would employ a young engineer in such frail health. Eventually, he came back to Britain and took a job in London, selling soap. But once more illness forced him to resign.

Baird Becomes an Inventor

His doctor advised him to leave London, with its smoke and fog, and try the softer cleaner air of the South Coast. So he went to Hastings. Here, while he paced along the shore and felt his strength gradually returning, he racked his brains as to how he was to earn his living. Here he was, an electrical engineer with a degree and with experience, but, while his brain was active and alert, his body could not stand up to the strain of regular work day after day. What was he to do? Perhaps he remembered his ill-fated glider. He had invented that—it might have worked. An inventor could work in his own time—not bound by office hours. He would invent.

But what would he invent? He remembered his old interest in photography, which had developed in his student days into an interest in the possibilities of seeing

Baird's original television apparatus (1925). A—the object. B—the revolving dial. C—the disc. E—the aperture to the light-sensitive cell

by electricity. He would go on from there.

Back in his seaside lodgings he started to build a model machine. He took as his basis the disc that Nipkow had invented, but he changed it by using one simple disc for both scanning and receiving the picture. He did not use a complicated picture, but only a small cross. The image of the cross was sent by a photo-electric cell through an amplifier to a receiving lamp. This glowed as the photo-electric cell received light through the holes in the disc. In front of the lowest hole, Baird put a small frame on which he calculated the image could be seen. To his great joy, this image was visible. His model worked. But it was made very largely of odd bits of material. He needed money if he was to develop his ideas.

Desperate situations require desperate action. Although his apparatus consisted of bits of cardboard and string, Baird decided to give a demonstration of his invention. As a demonstration it was a failure. Only one newspaper made any mention of it, but, by extraordinary good fortune, Baird's father saw the notice. He was so gratified at his son's achievement that he sent him £50.

Fifty pounds! With these riches, Baird hired a room as a workshop. Then he spent some of his money on an advertisement for an assistant. This was another fortunate move. The advertisement was seen by several scientists, who sent him friendly advice; among them was the Chief Engineer of the BBC.

It was clear to everyone that Baird's ideas were good, but not yet practical. However, encouraged by the notice and friendliness of fellow scientists, he moved back to London in 1924, to the relief of his landlord, who viewed his tenant's activities with considerable misgivings.

Demonstrations and Improvements

By another stroke of luck, soon after Baird was established in Soho, which was central and cheap as regards rents, the famous storekeeper, Gordon Selfridge, was on the lookout for some novelty to attract customers to the birthday-week celebrations of his shop in Oxford Street. He had heard of Baird and his invention, for it was his business to know about every new venture. He engaged the struggling scientist to show his model three times a day for a fee of £20 a week. The apparatus Baird used is now in the Science Museum in South Kensington.

The publicity that resulted from these demonstrations brought immediate help. Two electricity firms offered to supply him with valves and batteries equal to a gift of £200 from each, while his Scottish relations sent him £500 between them. Thus, with his fees from Selfridge, Baird was nearly £1,000 to the good.

He immediately tried to improve his pictures, working first with the ventriloquist's dummy he had used at Selfridges and then with an office boy from upstairs, who was bribed with half a crown to make scientific history by staying in the strong light which Baird's television equipment needed. So successful were these efforts that the inventor was able to give a further demonstration, this time to the Royal Institution and the Press. The good reception which his equipment received emboldened him to approach the BBC, in 1926, and ask for its help in transmitting his moving pictures over long distances. He managed to transmit a scene from his laboratory in Soho to the BBC studios, then in Savoy Hill (about a mile), and get it back on his receiver.

Next he applied to the Post Office for a licence to run an amateur television station. This was granted—No. 2 TV—and he was able to form a television

A television studio at 16, Portland Place, prior to the opening of the BBC's studios at Alexandra Palace

company. At last he had a real laboratory and was able to employ skilled assistants who understood long-distance radio transmissions. A wireless mast was erected over the laboratory in Leicester Square and pictures were successfully sent to Harrow, over ten miles away.

But Baird was not left alone to develop and enjoy his success. Stories of his activities spread all over the world and inspired other inventors to increase their efforts. An American company sent pictures over two hundred miles from Washington to New York. Baird countered with a transmission from London to Glasgow—four hundred miles. Then, as always, "thinking big", he aimed at sending his pictures across the Atlantic. This he did with the help of an enthusiastic television amateur in the United States. One of the subjects that Baird transmitted to the New World was a picture of himself!

By now companies with large financial resources were becoming interested in television, but Baird continued (with his relatively small company) to achieve ambitious projects, aiming at televising outdoor scenes with natural lighting and at coloured television. By 1928, the Bell Company in the USA beat him and achieved coloured television.

But, more important than the effect Baird had on his rivals overseas was the effect he had on the Post Office at home.

In the same year, 1928, the Postmaster-General officially acknowledged that television existed and, the next year, with the help of the BBC, Baird started an official though experimental television service. True, it was only received by about thirty enthusiasts, but Baird was full of hope when he watched his first programme—speeches by two scientists and "light entertainment" by three artistes. The pictures were described as being rather like those in automatic machines on piers and it looked as though television might follow the history of the film and, through the advertising performances at Selfridges and these small, dark programmes, become a kind of side-show at a fun fair.

Sound and Vision Together

But the parallel was not followed up—largely because of the serious interest of the BBC. In these first experimental programmes, the sound and picture were transmitted separately—sound first—since there was only one transmitter. The next year, there were two transmitters and sound and picture went out simultaneously. In 1930, the BBC, greatly daring, transmitted a play, and more receivers were bought as people began to think of television as something more than a temporary and passing fad of scientists. Spurred on by rivalry from America, Baird increased the size of his screen and redoubled his efforts for outdoor television. In 1931, he successfully televised the

A scene in the BBC television studio at Alexandra Palace (1937)

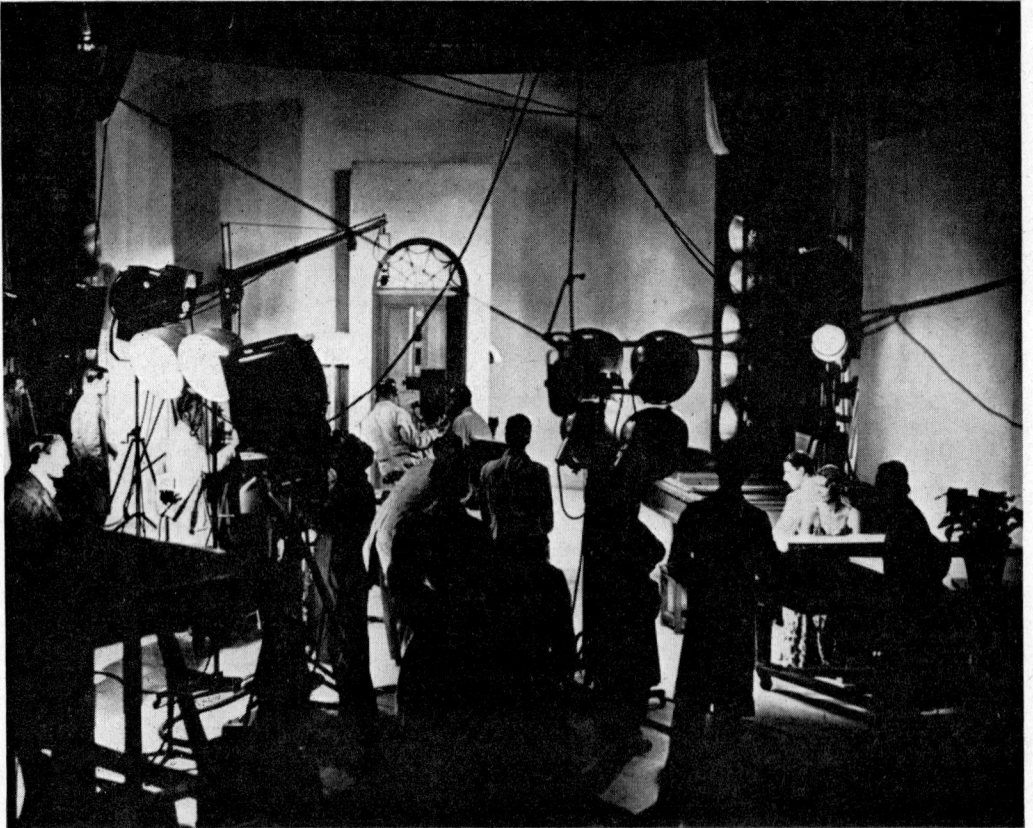

Derby, and this encouraged the BBC to put on programmes of its own, using Baird's apparatus. By the next year, when the Derby was televised a second time, 2,000 private television sets were ready to receive it. It was also projected on to a screen at the Metropole Cinema at Victoria in South London. One of the audience said that most of those present were not really impressed. They viewed it as a stunt and the picture seemed poor compared with the newsreel they would see that evening.

This was, perhaps, the first indication that television and films are fundamentally different.

Impressive or not, this televising of the Derby was a scientific triumph for Baird and perhaps the highest peak in his career. He was ahead of his rivals; he could see no basic weakness in his inventions. In 1932, the BBC decided not only to use Baird's equipment but engaged two of his staff to help transmit its own programmes under the supervision of a television research engineer. Four evenings a week, from 11 to 11.30, the programmes appeared regularly. The pictures were transmitted with only thirty lines at a rate of $12\frac{1}{2}$ frames a second. To get even a reasonable result, actors had to wear heavy make-up and the lighting had to be very strong indeed.

Even these concessions did not make the pictures good enough. The same difficulties were encountered by television in the USA, Italy, Austria and Germany. The apparatus was not really efficient, and people were beginning to tire of television, just as a novelty. The truth was that Nipkow's disc was not the right approach to the problem, but Baird and other pioneers stuck grimly to their methods of working and achieved 120 lines.

But this was still not good enough. If only he had looked up old copies of *Nature*, he would, perhaps, have realised how inspired was Swinton's suggestion about the value of the cathode-ray tube in the development of television.

A New Approach

Thirty years after Swinton put forward his ideas, a Russian, Zworykin, worked on the same lines, having first found out how to magnify very small electric currents. He had worked under the scientist Rosing when he was young and decided to emigrate to the USA, where he was employed by the Radio Corporation of America. He was given opportunities to experiment, and he perfected a cathode-ray camera, a project on which another American, Farnsworth, was also occupied in his own laboratory.

News of this new approach to television reached the BBC. A Government Committee was set up to decide which was the best system. After seven months, the Committee suggested the two systems should be used alternately; the cathode-ray tube system, perfected by the British EMI Company, should transmit programmes from the BBC Television Centre at Alexandra Palace (which had been opened in 1936) on one evening while Baird was to transmit on the next. Baird used 240 lines, but EMI produced 405 and could use four cameras in its one studio, switching from one to another to give a variety of picture-angle.

After only one year of competition there was no question as to which of the two systems was the better for practical transmission: that of EMI—although Baird had tried to simplify his method by televising film on a camera invented by Farnsworth. This choice of EMI was a bitter blow to Baird and his supporters. However, they did not give up their activities. Baird busied himself with colour television and the production of even wider screens.

Baird's electron camera (1937)

But when he died, in 1956, he was a sad and disappointed man.

In the Lead

The BBC now led the world in the field of television and put on all sorts of programmes. Development was so rapid that people forgot how recent an invention television was. Engineers concentrated particularly on improving their broadcasting of outside events (OB), such as the Boat Race, football, racing and tennis. By 1939, the programmes were so varied and so good that they attracted over 20,000 viewers.

On the advice of the Government Committee, the BBC abandoned the low definition of thirty lines and used high definition. The camera points its lens at a scene and the light from the objects in the scene is reflected on to the lens. Behind this is a cathode-ray tube, and by means of

this the light falls onto a tiny screen made up of photo-electric cells. These transmit electrical impulses which vary according to the strength of the light.

The scanning is done by 405 lines in one twenty-fifth of a second, the beam zigzagging across the picture and not going backwards and forwards horizontally. This scanning is called interlacing.

But with the outbreak of the Second World War in 1939, Britain, France, Austria, Italy, Holland, Sweden, Russia and Japan all stopped their television services, as these might have given information to the enemy. The United States was in a more fortunate position. Since television at this time only covered short distances, and America was far from the actual scene of the war and from hostile countries, her television service could be maintained without fear. This produced a situation similar to that which arose in the film world during the First World War. America was able to develop her

GLOBULES OF PHOTO
SENSITIVE MATERIAL

MICA
INSULATION

METAL
PLATE

TO AMPLIFIER

The photocell mosaic used as a screen in the television camera. The screen of such a camera is broken up into tiny dots, each of which acts as a separate photo-electric cell. This is arranged by means of a back plate of metal covered with mica insulation, on the front of which is a solution of photo-sensitive material, so placed that it becomes a mass of tiny globules. This material gives off electrons according to the intensity of the light which falls on it—more from the light areas of the picture than from the dark—and consequently each globule becomes positively charged to a greater or lesser degree. When the beam of negative electrons falls on them, therefore, they are discharged one after the other like condensers, causing variations of current in the metal plate. Thus the plate can send impulses of varying intensity through the ether in proper rotation, and the impulses can be built up at the other end (on your screen) into the same picture which sent them on their journey

industry while her rivals were checked by wartime conditions.

In 1946, the BBC renewed its television programmes, but by then its 405-line system was crude, compared with the 625 lines developed in the USA and adopted by countries in Europe, Asia and Africa which had started or restarted television after the war. Since then, various plans have been evolved to enable Britain to use the greater number of lines without making existing television sets useless and out of date.

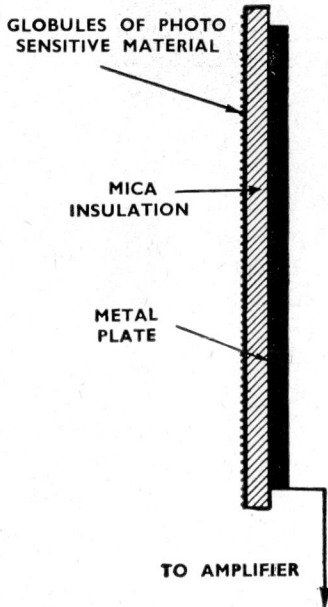

Independent Television

So popular did television become that in 1955 the Independent Television Authority (ITA) was set up by the Postmaster-General to provide a supplementary service to that of the BBC, which, until this date, had had a monopoly. The ITA builds transmission stations and leases them to companies which put on programmes that they pay for by transmitting advertising as well. The ITA supervises the companies very strictly. As it would be difficult for all the companies to produce worthwhile programmes to transmit during all the hours when television is permitted, they tend to use each other's programmes. This is called networking. However, each company produces a good deal of material with a local flavour.

Opinion is divided as to whether the monopoly of the BBC should have been challenged by Independent Television. However, writers, actors and technicians who have a varied market for their talents are in no doubt as to the value of the scheme and, probably, the competition between the two systems has encouraged variety, invention and initiative in both groups.

CHAPTER VIII

How Programmes reach the Television Screen

Now that television is an accepted part of our national life, nearly every home in Great Britain has a choice of programmes, from the BBC or from the ITA contracting company for the area. But how are these programmes produced and how do they reach our screens?

Actuality

John Logie Baird was right when he bent all his energies on televising the Derby. By this he achieved something different from any form of instruction or entertainment that had ever been known before. People saw the Derby at the moment when it was being run. This power of television to enable us to see far-away events when they are actually happening is its unique quality. A word has been coined to describe this—immediacy. It is this immediacy which makes television different from the theatre, lecture-room, concert hall, outdoor event or the cinema. In the first four cases you have to be on the spot to see what is happening; you, the actors, the lecturer, the orchestra, the team, are all at the same place at the same time. In the cinema you are away from home, present with the film, but the actors or the non-professional people who form part of the film are not there. Television unites you, at home, with the people who are actually in the scenes at the actual moment of the action. This is immediacy.

At first all the television plays, talks and competitions took place in a television studio, or were recorded by an outside broadcast. Each television studio that is built is more modern and has more advanced equipment than the last. The inventors are working so hard at improving television that a piece of equipment may easily be out of date within a year of its introduction.

The Granada Television Company has very well described its operations as being like an iceberg, of which a very small part is seen in the programmes, while the main part, the technical side, remains submerged or hidden away in the studios. This is true of all television.

The picture on the screen of a television receiver is produced by a spot of light of varying brightness. This moves across the screen from left to right and from top to bottom at the same time. This moving spot builds up twenty-five pictures per second as against the film's twenty-four; in Britain, it does this by drawing 405 lines on the screen for each picture. This adds up to 10,125 lines a second.

Essential Timing

It is essential that every television receiving set is working in time with the television cameras in the studios which are transmitting the 10,125 lines a second. It is the job of studio engineers (who are called rack-men) to make certain that this happens and that cameras and receivers are working together, or "in synchronisation", shortened to "in synch". The problem is to make certain that every set stops the line of electrical impulses at the same time and prevents it running on to the next transmitted line. What happens is that a signal is transmitted from the studios to your set saying, "That line is finished. Start the next." This signal is sent in various ways, but it is absolutely essential if the picture sent from the studio is to be correctly picked up by television sets all over the country. For this reason, the engineers in charge of synchronisation are far more important than any television star. They really take the place of the laboratories which develop and print film in the film world. They can alter the lighting of pictures and are really creative artists as well as technicians.

To ask, "How is a television programme put on the air?" is rather like asking "How long is a piece of string?" There is no answer to either question.

The work that goes into producing a television programme varies from country to country and, in Britain, between the BBC and the different independent companies. However, there is a general pattern which is followed or adapted in most cases, according to the type of programme.

Immediacy is well demonstrated by this picture of the annual ceremony of Trooping the Colour

The Producers

Many large television companies divide their programmes among producers, who are responsible for what goes on the air in their special kind of television: the Drama Producer, the Light Entertainment Producer, the Documentary Producer, the Outside Broadcasts Producer and so on. In a small company one producer may be responsible for more than one type of programme. Together with the heads of his company, the producer decides on a general policy for his programmes and then his word is law. Under him work several directors and, if he is clever, he employs different kinds of men and women so that the programmes they direct under his supervision may be as varied as possible and not the same old material rehashed over and over again.

The Writer and the Director

Next comes the story or, in the case of a documentary or a quiz programme, the pattern of entertainment that will be followed. Usually the company has a number of writers working for it and they will naturally be chosen for their individual styles. So it will be possible to find a writer who specialises in comedy or in adventure or in social studies—a writer who will suit the subject

The television camera-man in action

The complexity of a studio in which various different sets—each with their own network of lights—are ready to enable the scene to change without any time-lag appearing on the television screen

of the programme. This subject may be an original idea sent to the company or an idea the staff work up themselves, or the adaptation of a book or a stage play.

The writer and director work closely together and both are influenced by the amount of money available for the programme. The money must be spent wisely so that it shows on the screen, and not be wasted on, say, six hundred horse-men who are only seen for half a minute.

The Set and the Cast

Once the story is under way, two other persons are called in. The first is the designer who will plan the sets. He is influenced by which studio he has to use, because in a large studio he can design more and larger sets. He arranges them so that the actors, the cameras and the microphone booms can move easily from one set to another as the scenes follow each other in the script. He and the writer, too, are influenced by the numbers of cameras available. If there are six cameras with plenty of camera cranes put at the director's disposal, then complicated sets on two levels can be planned. Too much equipment in a small studio, however, is more of a drawback than a limited amount of equipment, for staff and actors cannot move about easily if the floor space is congested with cables and machines.

The second person who is called in early is the casting director. He or she suggests actors to the director and finally makes arrangements with them to appear in the programme. Here again money is important and it is better to have a play or entertainment with a few good actors than with a whole crowd who are competent, but not outstanding. It is not as easy to engage actors for television as it is for films, for they often agree to appear once only. Then, if the programme is ever repeated, they have to agree to appear again on being paid a second fee. Often, too, they have to be re-engaged if the programme is sold overseas.

When the actors have been cast, they consult with the director, with the designer and with the wardrobe-mistress about their clothes. Obviously, what they wear must contrast with the set, or they would not be seen; on the other hand, their clothes must not clash with the curtains or furniture. It is important, too, that what they wear suits the character they are portraying.

At this point, the hairdresser and wigmaker may be consulted, especially if the story is historical and needs costume and wigs.

Meanwhile, the script has been completed and analysed. This means that lists are made of things that must be on the set (called properties). It is the job of the property-master to see that jugs of water, cushions, books and other things necessary for the action are available and suitable. In this he works with the designer, who also usually chooses the furniture.

A television script never has the same details of camera movement as a film script, for the final camera action and the transition from long to medium or close shot is the concern of the director on the set.

Music and Sound Effects

To help him, the director has one or more production assistants (PAs) and one or more secretaries. One of their jobs is to make contact with the music department. The head of this department is told how much music will be needed and of what kind. The music may be specially written for the programme, but more often it is taken off gramophone records. The director chooses the music he wants from the material suggested to him and then the head of the music department has not only to see that it is available in the studio, but also that he has permission to use it and has paid for the right to do so to the owner of the copyright. The rights to use music are as complicated as the agreements with actors. There may also be sound effects for the programme: galloping horses, the beating of waves or the sound of a cock crowing. Large television companies have their own sound libraries, but, if a very unusual sound is needed, they may have to buy it from another television company or from a film company. Sounds may be on gramophone records or on film. The music and sounds have to be arranged in order, so that the director may bring them into his programme at the right moment.

A famous actor, Charles Laughton, faces the television camera

Filming and Rehearsing

Although most of the programme will be produced in the studio, the director may need some pieces of film to show his characters getting into cars and driving away, hurrying along the streets of Paris, or climbing a mountain. Some television companies have their own film units who take these film "inserts" under the supervision of the director or one of his PAs. However, many use an outside film company which contracts to do the work. Filming for television has a special technique. The pictures require a different exposure and different lighting from films taken for showing in cinemas. The special shape of the television screen has also to be remembered when the pictures are composed.

The programme can be rehearsed for as much as six weeks or, in the case of a quiz programme, as little as a couple of days. As the television studios are always in demand for live transmissions they cannot be spared for rehearsals. Most television studios have rehearsal rooms, but there are often not enough to go round. So rehearsals take place in drill halls or church rooms. The sets are marked on the floor, usually with coloured sticky tape, and the artists have to imagine the scenery and furniture. It is a wonderful sight to see an actor intent on his performance, seriously climbing up a non-existent staircase. For them, Shakespeare's exhortation, "Let your imaginary forces work", is well-timed.

For final rehearsals with sets, properties, lights, cameras and microphone booms, the production unit and cast move into the studio for as long before the transmission as the space can be spared for this particular production. No wonder, very occasionally, one can see a microphone that should be safely out of the picture— or the camera sometimes fails to find and focus an actor. But this sort of accident is, nowadays, very rare, and—interestingly enough—is seldom resented by viewers. They accept such occasional lapses as the price of immediacy.

Lighting

The lighting director works with the director, the picture controller and the cameramen to arrange his lights once the action is planned. The pattern of lighting is set up on a lighting panel and the lamps are switched on to each set as a whole unit when they are wanted, never lamp by lamp, as in a film studio. Thus, when the lighting is agreed, it can never go wrong and be delayed.

Before the transmission, one or two dress rehearsals are held. The actors are made up by the make-up team and work for the first time in the hot lights. The man in charge of the studio floor is called the floor manager, and his word on the floor is law. The director speaks to him and he transmits instructions to the camera and sound crews, and often to the actors. He is responsible for order and discipline and he can often be heard roaring, "Quiet, please!"

Editing the Programme

The director sits in a control-room apart from the studio, but with a window into it. Before him are as many screens as there are cameras—perhaps six—and on yet another screen he can view lengths of film that are being introduced into the production as well, and on another any still pictures. Beside him sits a "vision-mixer", who cuts from one picture to another at his instructions, as the play proceeds. The PA often hands on these instructions and carefully times the production. Camera I may give a long shot, Camera II show action on another set, Camera III a closer view of the set-up of

The production lighting control-room. The tools with which these men work include the script, monitoring sets, a complicated lighting plot and, most important of all, skill and experience which enables them to make quick, effective decisions on the spot

Camera I, and so on. The director edits his action while it goes on, just as a film editor edits scenes in the peace of the cutting-room, after they have been filmed, developed and printed.

The film editor can try different arrangements but the television director can do no such thing. His is an exhausting job, calling for clearness of mind and quick decision for, once a mistake has been made, there is no way of going back and correcting it. The picture as the vision-mixer cuts it appears on your screen. The sound-mixer sits in a special cubicle together with his "effects" man. He has his own highly sensitive loud-speaker. He must be in a silent place to judge his sound, for in the control-room the director may be giving instructions all the time through the short-wave radio to

the floor manager as well as to the vision-mixer and to the PA. The sound-mixer mixes the sounds from the studio with the music or natural effects as the director has instructed. In other words, the sound is edited on the spot too. But while the director is giving artistic instructions to members of his camera team with their equipment, the cameras are controlled as well, from the technical point of view, in the control-room, so that the pictures they transmit are of the highest possible quality. In the same way, the light from the studio lamps is perpetually checked, as is the quality of the sound. In fact, two controls are always at work in the studio—the technical and the creative. Television viewers and critics are too apt to concentrate on the actor who is on the set and to forget the teams of technicians

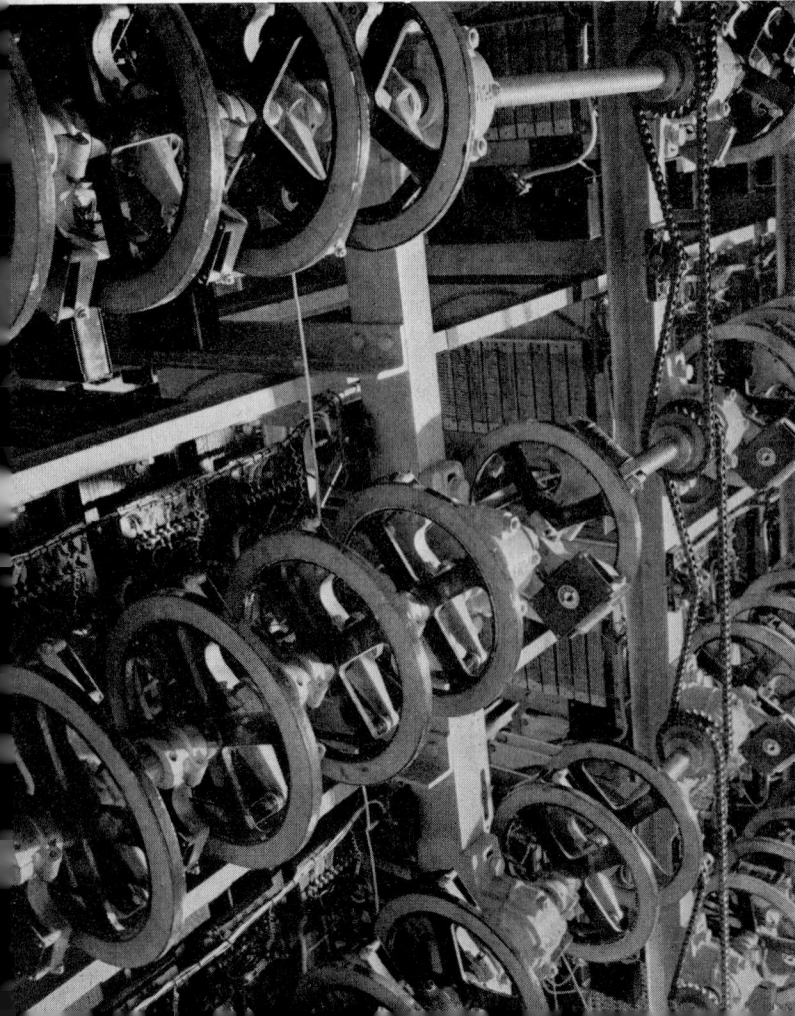

Electro-magnetic clutch assemblies in the dimmer room of the television studio

The quiet domestic scene which appears on your television screen is, in fact, a minute part of this studio

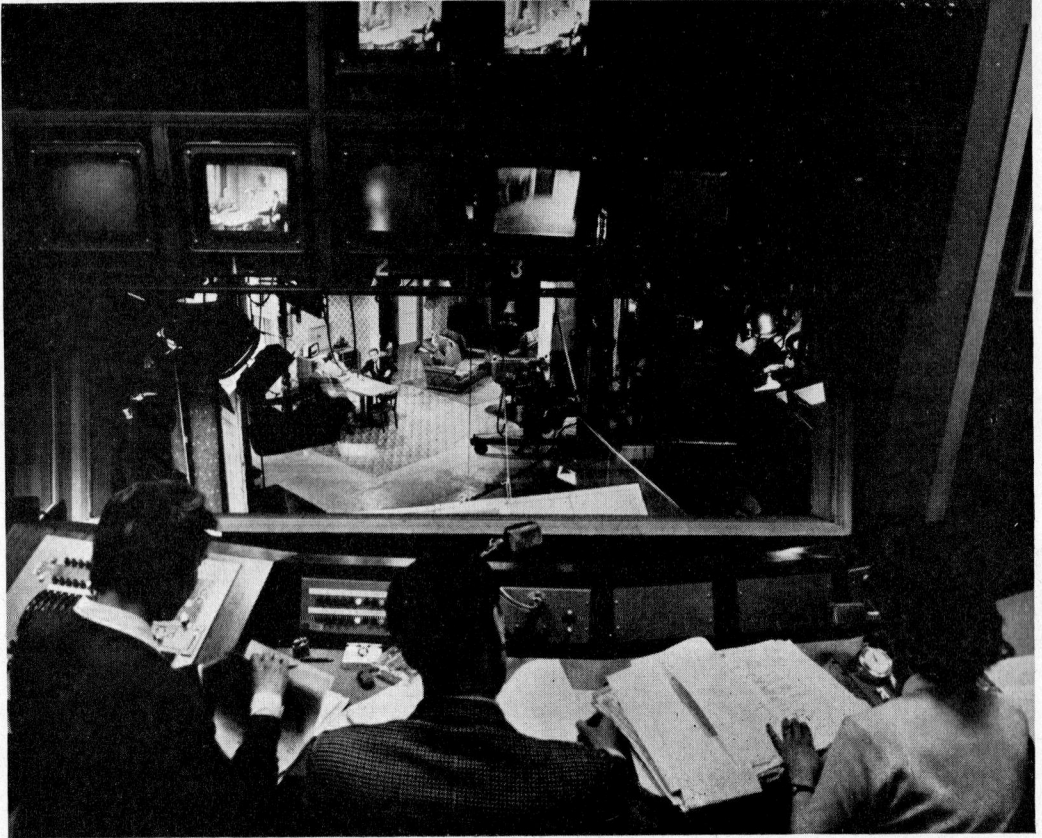

A view of the set as seen from the control room

who are concentrating on bringing his image on to the television screen in the family living-room.

Outside Broadcasts

The production of an outside broadcast of, say, a football match or of the Olympic Games is based on the same principle as that of the play or programme from the studio, but even more difficult. The director surveys the scene of activity and decides where he can best site his cameras and microphones. There can be no rehearsal, but he tells his team what he hopes to get in the way of pictures, and relies very much on their discretion and powers of improvisation. Who, for in-

stance, can tell where a football will go on the field, or from which point and when a goal will be kicked? Instead of the control-room, there is a van, fitted up with all the necessary equipment, but it is compressed into a very small space. The director communicates with his team by radio as in the studio, but often they are much farther away. The technical problem is how to get the pictures from an outside broadcast, or OB as it is called, back to the studio where synch., light and sound can be controlled. This is done by a system of "hops" from one temporary short-wave radio station to another. These stations are set up on high ground so that the very high radio frequencies of

The vision control room

the television cameras can travel in straight lines from the place of the OB to the studio. It requires great skill to plan where to put these radio stations with the most efficiency and economy and, often, they are sited on the tops of lonely hills or desolate moors. However, the problem is not as serious as it used to be, for the BBC and ITA engineers now have a pretty good idea of the best places to put their radio links between any sports centre and the nearest studio. Programmes can also be transmitted over a land-line through arrangement with the GPO.

The engineers, technical staff, production staff and actors and, probably, people who take part in television competitions and quizzes enjoy the immediacy of these "live" studio programmes and of the outside broadcasts. They feel the excitement of the unseen audience and this provides some of the stimulation that actors and stage staff get from the presence of a live audience in a theatre, music-hall

Outside broadcast—televising spectacular events at the Coventry Air Pageant

or concert hall. In a film studio, on the other hand, there is no audience and there is no sense of immediacy. A scene can be shot and re-shot until it is right and, in place of stimulation from an audience, all those taking part have the inner stimulation of being able to go on and on until they have done their best. Immediacy is very important to those who work in television and also to viewers who appreciate something special in its quality. But, from the point of view of television management, it is wasteful to have first-class television programmes and not be able to repeat them. Efforts have therefore been made to record and store television programmes.

Recording and Storage

The coming of commercial television and the introduction of advertisements made some form of pre-recording and replaying essential. For instance, all advertisements have to be most carefully checked to pass the requirements of the ITA before they can appear on the television screen. They are, therefore, all filmed. At one time, it was thought that all television programmes should be filmed in advance, but this idea was soon given up, for it took too long to process the film and was too expensive as well. However, some programmes that cannot be obtained in any other way, such as Nature or travel programmes, underwater programmes and some of the serials of the Western type, which demand a great deal of out-of-door action and fights, are still filmed. Fights can only be made convincing by film editing, since very few television stars can take part in violent battles of fisticuffs and

Immediacy at Silverstone

gymnastic feats of violence with conviction, nor indeed are they willing to do so. Filmed programmes are transmitted by the television camera scanning each frame as the film passes before it.

It is possible to make a record of live studio and OB transmissions by making a film record of the television pictures, and this is called a tele-recording. However, the main objection to this method of storing programmes was, and still is, the loss of quality in the picture, which, when it is transmitted, becomes a copy of a copy of a programme.

New Processes

Only a short time ago, a new development was perfected which is called video-tape. This wonderful discovery, which originated in the USA, is a method of recording on to a magnetic tape the electrical impulses that make up the picture and sound of a television transmission. Although, in principle, it is the same as recording sounds on a tape-recorder, it is infinitely more complex, because the picture has to be recorded too. It is accomplished by using a magnetic tape two inches wide, which passes through

a machine at fifteen inches per second, recording the electrical impulses on tracks which are perpendicular to the tape and which can receive recordings of both sound and picture. Video-tape machines are installed in studios and OB units and are invaluable in storing programmes. The main advantage of the tape is that it needs no processing and can be played again at once. For instance, a video-tape of a prize-fight in the USA was flown by jet 'plane to Britain and shown on BBC television in less than eighteen hours. It is reassuring to everyone taking part in a transmission to know that, if a programme is being recorded on video-tape, a major disaster—such as an actor fainting—can be overcome by a retake and, since video-tape can be cut and joined, smaller mistakes, such as a complete drying up on lines, can be cut and a retake put in. However, retakes on video-tape are not encouraged. No studio time has been allotted for them—they remove the sense of immediacy and they are still relatively slow and expensive to accomplish.

Video-tape can never be regarded as a replacement of film, which is such a malleable medium, but its use for record-

A science lesson being broadcast on closed circuit television

A combination of two techniques: by means of a small television camera attached to the film camera, the director and client can see how this commercial will appear when it is transmiitted

ing and storing programmes does enable studios to be used all day instead of only at transmitting hours and, because of its introduction, actors who are playing in a theatre at night can take part in programmes in the mornings or afternoons. In other words, video-tape makes television less rigid and less confined by time and place. In addition, a new method of recording on plastic is now being developed.

Television is being used increasingly for education by closed circuit—that is, by a television system working in one or two buildings only, and not over the air. Surgical operations can be shown in various lecture-rooms of hospitals, and several classes can watch and listen to one lecturer. In Britain, in March 1961, one Middlesex science master gave a lesson which was followed in his school and in another two miles away—both

sets of pupils being able to ask questions by means of short-wave radio. Television is also used to see where men cannot go—to look under the sea, in atomic piles and in missiles in orbit around the earth.

Soon, it is hoped, television will be transmitted across the Atlantic and, when we consider how quickly television has developed, we could hardly be surprised at such a development. Yet careless use of a television set, failure to tune it properly, a vacuum-cleaner in the next room, an electric lift nearby, a passing car in the street with no suppressor, can ruin the television picture. Many technicians and creative artists have struggled and are struggling to transmit programmes for your enjoyment and instruction. They work in vain if you do not see that your television set and those of your neighbours can and do work properly.

CHAPTER IX

The Film in the Age of Television

By 1962, television will have reached twelve million homes in Great Britain and Northern Ireland. Soon a point of saturation will be reached, and the regular rate of expansion which has put over a million new receivers in our homes each year will become a steady turn-over representing replacement of old sets rather than an increase in the number of homes where television is available. But during this period of expansion, which developed on an ever-increasing scale once the BBC had started its regular transmissions again in 1946, and was accelerated even more when commercial television began in 1955, the prosperity of the cinema receded. The cinema now has to compete with some 140 hours of television entertainment (BBC and Independent) each week. A third of our original total of some 4,700 cinemas represents the proportion of theatres that have already closed or are scheduled to be closed, while audiences are estimated for the 1960's at a level well below half what they were in 1947 before television began to get its hold upon the public.

For the film-maker the position is somewhat different. Some studios have been closed as redundant—that is true. Others are increasingly giving up space to the production of films designed for television, the series of half-hour stories which are made in large quantities for showing at home and for export, particularly to the United States and the Commonwealth countries. Ealing Studios, once a stronghold for the best in British film-making for the cinemas, has now become the centre for television film production for the BBC. Many film-makers have joined the staffs of the television studios. For the film-maker, in fact, television represents a further outlet for his work rather than a direct threat to his employment. Even if he finds himself making commercials instead of documentaries, cartoons or even features, he is still making films, even though he may not particularly like what he is making!

For the film producer, determined to keep in business and serve the public through the cinemas, the period has been exceptionally difficult. Most countries outside the communist group still depend to greater or less extent on importing American films to maintain a constant change of programme for their audiences. Few countries meet even as much as one-third or one-half of their needs through local production; in Britain the proportion of British films to imported ones shown in our cinemas is approximately one-third only. Therefore the effects of television on the American film industry were and still are bound to be reflected in any industry outside America that continues to rely for the greater part of its film entertainment on what the Americans produce.

New Attractions

This is particularly true of Britain.

A composite photograph showing the advantages of CinemaScope using 55 mm. film. 1. The images are radiantly bright. 2. The background is clearly in focus and the feeling of audience participation is emphasised. 3. There is a considerable illusion of depth. 4. There is no distortion when viewed from any angle

When television first began to empty the cinemas, producers in the United States grasped hurriedly and uncertainly at half-developed techniques of three-dimensional cinematography (3-D), but these failed lamentably both in America and Britain to attract a permanent public; eye-strain, dislike of wearing the polarised spectacles in the cinema, but above all the disappointment in the dramatic effectiveness of 3-D soon led to this experiment being abandoned just at the very time when the technique itself was, in fact, perfected.

The third dimension was rapidly followed by the wide-screen systems, which broke up the old standardisation of picture dimension into four main shapes: the giant screen (such as Cinerama), standard wide-screen (such as Cinema-Scope), normal screen (itself widened to a ratio of about 1·6 to 1 as compared with the ratio in the early 1950's of 1·3 to 1), and the ratio required for normal substand projection and for television, which remains 1·3 to 1. These changes have led to the introduction of many patented systems with their appropriate lenses and cameras, and have forced both producers and exhibitors to invest considerable sums of money in order to adapt themselves to these variations in screen. Similarly, the larger theatres have had to install equipment which enables them to reproduce multi-channelled magnetic sound.

None of these innovations, with all the artistic problems that accompany their effective use for the story-telling that still remains the principal function of the entertainment film, was initially asked for by the leading writers, directors, cameramen or actors working in the cinema. What, in fact, happened followed exactly the pattern of the introduction of sound. The screen, whether merely larger or considerably wider, seemed at first horrible! Then the more enterprising film-makers accepted these bigger, wider screens and began to show how they might be used to advantage— for spectacle, as in *The Robe*, or for more intimate subjects, as in Elia Kazan's *East of Eden*, or even for both, as in such films as George Stevens' *Giant* or Stanley Donen's musical, *Seven Brides for Seven Brothers*. Just as Shakespeare made great drama in the unpromising circumstances of an open stage in an uncovered theatre, with a noisy rabble for his audience, so the film-maker accepted the wide-screen and made a good best of it. The old small screens were soon called postage-stamps, and forgotten. Perhaps they began to look too like television!

Telling a Good Story Well

Having tried to entice the public back to the cinemas with wide-screen and again failed after the first sensationalism was over, the producers reverted to the real business of the cinema—telling a good story well. At the same time Hollywood itself began to change its function. As in Britain, the studios began slowly to turn to the enemy, television, and to make films in series which, in the case of America, developed into a flood. Films for the cinema began to be drastically reduced in number, most of them being made by independent producers in some form of financial association with the big production or distribution companies. In other words, at the very time when the mass production of films for television came to the forefront

in Hollywood, a much more highly individual form of production was adopted as the most satisfactory way of making films for what might be called the new cinema.

The new cinema is the cinema that has to face having an active competitor in the home. During the 1950's television, which revolutionised entertainment for Britain and America, developed much more slowly in other, less industrialised countries. It came more slowly and with far less impact to such countries as France and Italy, both of which had advanced and highly productive film industries. For many countries the revolution that happened rapidly during the 1950's in America and Britain was to come more gradually during the latter part of the 1950's and the earlier part of the 1960's.

Television is by no means universal yet; many nations either have none at all, have it only experimentally for a very few hours a week, or have it in too expensive a form for receivers to be purchased by the public as a whole. Therefore, in many parts of the world, the cinema remains still the most popular form of entertainment, immune for a little while longer from competition. On the other hand, in the communist countries television is well advanced, but, because it, like the cinema, is State-controlled, there is only technical competition between the two. Even so, the films now being made in the Soviet Union have become much more human, more dramatic, more conscious that they must be attractive to a changing public than they were in the days when the cinema was the only mass entertainment available, apart from the living theatre. This change in appeal is, no doubt, also due to a changing attitude to entertainment itself in the Soviet Union since the discrediting of Stalin. Russian films, though still preoccupied with showing people as happy and contented within a community which is communist, are also prepared to deal far more than they were before with the complications in the private lives of their principal characters. This was the case with the film *The Cranes are Flying* and even more in the astonishing films made in Poland by the young film-maker Andrzej Wajda, who is not afraid to reveal the distress and perplexity of his far from simple characters.

Foreign-language Films

With the shortage of films from the American producers, the cinemas in Britain have been faced with a problem of how to keep their screens filled. One solution was to introduce, gradually and carefully, a few films from countries with a different language—films which may, indeed, be dubbed (that is, re-tracked) in English, but for the most part depend on printed sub-titles. Previously these had only been shown at a few specialised cinemas, followed by a secondary distribution to film societies. This widening of interest in the public has been accompanied by the popularisation of foreign stars, such as Sophia Loren, Anna Magnani, Gina Lollobrigida and Yves Montant in American and British films. Similarly, on the Continent, there has been a great increase in co-production, that is, producers from two countries, such as France and Italy, pooling the costs of production and making a film simultaneously, in two languages, with stars popular in both countries. In fact, during recent years the film industries of America, France, Britain, Italy and West Germany in particular have become increasingly interlocked. Britain now earns more money from her best films overseas than she earns at home; American producers are constantly making films in Britain, France, Italy, in fact on location all over the world so that Hollywood seems only a base from which the American film-making campaign is launched. This is partly

Fernandel in The Little World of Don Camillo, *Italy/France (1952)*

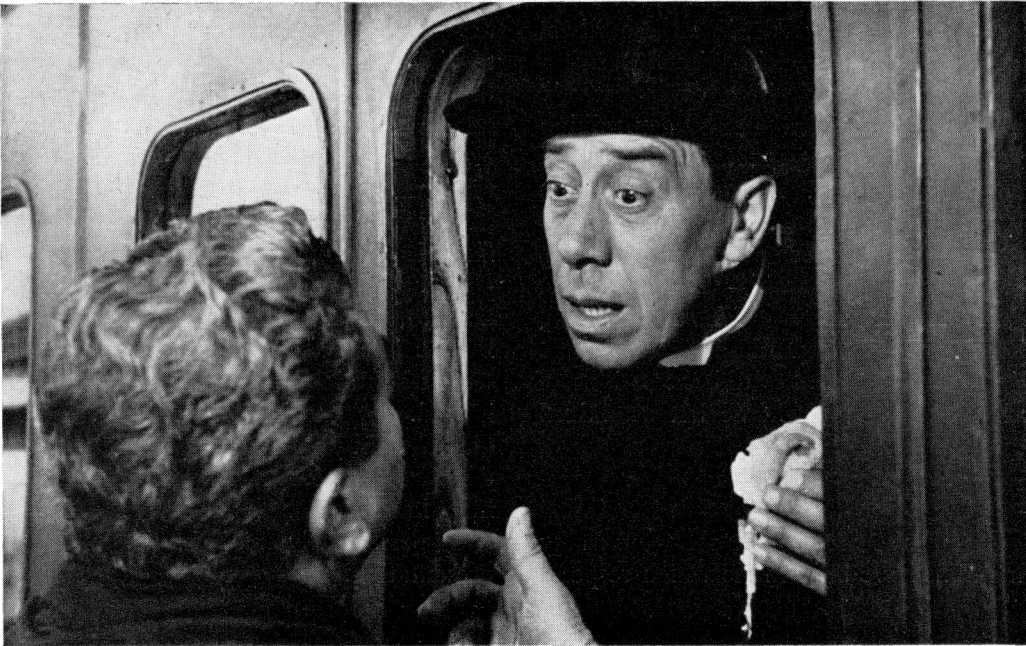

explained by the fact that film-making is much cheaper outside America than it is inside; but also the varied landscapes of the world and the rich resources of extra stories and foreign acting talent are available to producers prepared to work abroad and make films on such a spectacular scale that television is for a while forgotten and the public begin to patronise in large numbers the cinemas that offer them scenery on the grand scale, sensational action, vast sets and even vaster crowds, as well as international casts of well-known actors and actresses. This is a paradox. Never before have the successful films been so unsuccessful, playing to empty cinemas while the public watch television, go dancing or crowd into sporting events. Similarly, never before has the unusual film been so well patronised in the more specialised theatres.

More Money for Fewer Films

Producers have reacted to this situation in various ways. The first is to spend more money on a few pictures. *Ben-Hur* cost some five million pounds, but it seemed that it could run for years. *The Bridge on the River Kwai* (an American production with a British director) cost a great sum, but within a comparatively short while had been seen by 235 million people. The great spectacle films, *The Ten Commandments*, *Around the World in Eighty Days*, *Spartacus*, *The Guns of Navarone* and not a few others, were all designed for long runs and world-wide audiences. Few if any of them will make a loss, whereas many a small and cheaply-made picture relying on the old attractions of crime or romance will be left unnoticed by the public.

The "New Wave"

During the past five or six years many fine films have been made which respond to the new cinema's need for films that present the public with screen-plays reflecting an altogether better judgment of human values than those that are based on sensationalism. They have come from many countries—from Japan, for instance, in the films of Kurosawa, from India in the films of Satyajit Ray, from Poland in the films of Wadda, from Italy in the films of de Sica. Certain of the young directors working in what has been called the "new wave" in France have produced films which are enlightening and exciting— films such as *Les Quatre Cents Coups*. In Britain the best of the initial films in this new style was *Saturday Night and Sunday Morning*, while from America have come outstanding films such as *The Defiant Ones*, *A Man is Ten Feet Tall* and *Shadows* (all dealing with race relations), and rather more sensational but still remarkable films, such as *Anatomy of a Murder* and *Inherit the Wind* (dealing with justice in American society).

What matters in all these films is the degree of honesty with which human relationships are shown; the capacity of writer, director and actor to understand the society in which their characters have to live. Films should be judged from this point of view just as strictly as novels and plays. The costs of production are obviously incomparably greater than those involved in either publishing or the presentation of plays in the theatre, and therefore financial considerations constantly force producers to compromise in their attitude both to their stories and their characters. But an influential film will in the end be seen by audiences which are very great indeed. What it has to say, either directly or by implication, is therefore all the more important, especially since the film has become by now so powerful and persuasively real in its technical presentation.

CHAPTER X

Types of Programmes: Cinema and Television

ALTHOUGH THE cinema and television both entertain and inform the public be means of moving pictures, the kinds of programme they put on are very different.

Early television programmes were always very short—lasting for not more than half an hour. This was because it was difficult to guarantee that the equipment would continue to function and because the lights were so strong that actors and speakers, as well as the floor staff, were soon completely burnt out, if not tired out. In the same way, early films, like *Rescued by Rover* or the Chaplin comedies, were only ten or twenty minutes long.

Television Serials

During the war, when European television was in abeyance, television went ahead in the USA, where practically all programmes were "sponsored"—that is, paid for by an advertiser. To persuade the public to view regularly and so to see the advertisements, serial stories or series of stories dealing with one or two characters, became the fashion. These were usually made in sets of thirteen or multiples of thirteen because the year is made up of four sets of thirteen weeks. Each lasted half an hour, minus the time for the advertisements, which works out at about $27\frac{1}{2}$ minutes. After the war,

first the BBC and then the ITA companies needed to fill up their programmes with ready-made material from the USA, or which they could produce jointly with the USA companies. Then Canada and Australia had the same urgent need for ready-made programme material and acquired these existing programmes. So the pattern of the half-hour series or serial was adopted in most English-speaking countries and adapted by others. Indeed, nowadays, if a television company wants world distribution for its television programmes it is more or less forced to accept this pattern.

Early Film Serials

At the beginning of its activities, the film industry, too, produced a great number of serials and series. People in their sixties still remember the thrills of the *Exploits of Elaine* and the *Shielding Shadow* or the fascination of the natural history stories in *Secrets of Nature*. But the change in the length of feature films and the convention of the two-feature programme squeezed out the serials and the "interest" series. Now only a few Western serials are made for the cinema in the USA, but the Children's Film Foundation in Britain produced a steady flow of serials, including the first coloured serials. Perhaps now, with serials so popular on television, it is too late for the film industry to try serials again and compete on its wide screens.

Some very enlightened advertisers in the USA were and are ready to pay for a different kind of programme. As a result, some excellent concerts, documentary programmes, plays and talks were also produced in North America, and set a pattern for the rest of the world to copy, to vary or to improve. In the USA a company that wants to advertise its goods on television pays for the time of its advertisement on the screen and for the programme that comes out afterwards under its name. It does, to a great extent, control the programme. In Britain, on ITA, an advertiser can only buy time for a short advertisement, the length of which is limited by law. It has no influence on the programmes that come before or after it. These are produced at the expense and on the initiative of the television company which acts under the control of the Independent Television Authority.

Immediacy

The quality of immediacy affects many types of television programmes. There is a good deal of news reporting and sports reporting and, in this field of information, the film newsreels have been almost completely superseded. Then there are magazine programmes, some daily and some weekly, which consist of reports from on the spot, dealing with subjects of topical but not of such immediate interest as to be "news". The great feature both of television news and of television magazine programmes is the interviews with people on the spot. All sorts of people appear on the television screen and relate what they saw or what they think, and they often reveal how very little they observed or actually know. When this sort of interviewing started, people were shy and reluctant to talk when approached by the television interviewer, but now most people are used to the idea and talk glibly into the proferred microphone. About twenty years ago film documentaries started interviews with non-actors, but the fashion died out for reasons that are open to argument—chiefly because, perhaps, film audiences were impatient of immediacy and its lack of polish.

Other immediate television programmes are competitions, brains-trusts and quizzes. Their attraction, again, lies in the fact that we view them as they happen. We see people, like ourselves, now, at this very moment, taking part in programmes, being successful, being gay or making fools of themselves. Very few people do the latter. Those who have the daring to take part in such programmes are usually people of character who are well able to stand up to the searching eye of the camera. Indeed, it is their portrayal of real characters that gives these programmes their main attraction. It is difficult to pretend to be other than you are on the television screen, as many politicians have learned to their cost.

A scene from Rescued by Rover

So, too, intellectual men and women, some of whom insist on lecturing to the television camera instead of speaking into it confidentially, fail to make contact with the tiny, individual groups which make up the huge audience at home. Reputations have been made or broken by television and some people, such as the newscasters and compères who might never have been heard of outside their immediate family circle, have become household names. Film programmes have never achieved this easy co-operation with the man in the street, probably because film production, even newsreel and documentary production, aims at such perfection that the ordinary person is intimidated, and the quality of reality gets lost.

Length and Concentration

To compete with television, feature films have got longer and longer, so that some last over two hours. Whether audiences can concentrate so long is a question to which no one yet knows the answer. But television programmes seldom last more than an hour. Even then, the close concentration that looking at a small screen demands means that viewers often lose the thread of the programme through mental exhaustion unless the script has allowed for this. Here we possibly find one reason for the popularity of the Western. At intervals we can relax and watch the chase after the mail-coach or the routine fight in the bar-room, without having to worry about a plot. Probably the problem of concentration

Televising the BBC news—the newscaster must be on the alert for last-minute items

for a long time on the television screen explains the popularity of variety programmes which are made up of a number of short turns and do not demand a sustained interest.

Musicals also enable viewers to relax from time to time, in the cinema as well as in the theatre and at home looking at television. Ballets and dances in musicals are planned for filming or television, and are far more satisfactory than any attempts to televise or film live ballet. The reason for this is that ballets on the stage are planned to be viewed as a whole and cannot be divided into sections. But cameras —to give variety on the screen—must switch arbitrarily from one dancer or group of dancers to another, though viewers may wish to look at another section of the dance or the complete stage. The dances and ballets on film and television have been deliberately composed in sections and not to be viewed as a whole, and so are completely satisfying to the eye.

Cartoons and puppet stories made for the cinema come over well on television, but far better are the programmes of this nature prepared especially for television and allowing for the limits of the television screen. Again, very talented performers who manipulate and talk to puppets have had an opportunity to develop their art on television when there was no scope for them in the live theatre or on films.

Natural History

Nature programmes are very popular on television, but the limits of black-and-white pictures make them far less attractive than similar programmes in the cinema. But, with a few exceptions, very few Nature films can be included in current film programes, because a Nature film is seldom long enough to fill a whole programme, and costs too much to be worth making as a short, supporting picture. Nature programmes on television are always filmed first, because one cannot guarantee that the birds and the beasts will give a "live" performance. The close-ups are usually good, but the longer shots seldom have the same rich quality as good film on a film projector. Television audiences, however, are nothing like as critical as film audiences with regard to the quality of the pictures and this tolerance is not limited to viewers of Nature programmes.

News, documentaries, panels and games, magazines, cartoons and puppets, competitions, serials, series, plays—all these types of programme appear regularly on our television screens. Feature films with supporting short "interest" films and cartoons are the material offered by the cinemas. It may well be that the two arts—film and television—are already staking out their spheres of influence and each will tend to concentrate on the type of programme it is most suited to produce.

Twenty frames from the Halas and Batchelor cartoon series for television. Twenty-five of these frames represent one second of Foo Foo

CHAPTER XI

The Effects of Television on the Cinema

TELEVISION EVERYWHERE has had a marked effect on the film industry. However, it is important to remember that changes in the film world were due to occur, even if there had been no television sets installed in our homes. Of course, in countries where there is no television, films retain their popularity and financial success, though there are fewer films generally available.

By 1939, in Britain and other Western countries, many cinemas were already in need of repair or were so old-fashioned that they were due to be closed up. But the war meant that from 1939 to 1944 there was very little entertainment available, other than films, either for the troops or for exhausted civilians. As a result, there was a boom in films; people were willing to watch almost any moving picture and they were prepared to put up with uncomfortable theatres—they were better than air-raid shelters or bomb-damaged homes.

After the war, conditions changed. Homes became better furnished and decorated and more comfortable. The local cinema no longer seemed the height of luxury and modern design. The rising cost of building made it difficult to renovate or rebuild cinemas and, for some time, until war shortages ended, it was impossible to replace worn-out projectors and sound equipment. Audiences found their film theatres less attractive in every way.

Post-war Developments

The old cinemas had been built in the middle of towns near railway stations and bus terminals, so that people travelling by public transport could reach them easily. But, after the war, more and more people travelled in their own cars and the cinemas had only small car-parks, if they had any at all. Patrons had to park a long way away and walk, perhaps in the rain, to the cinema. They became more and more unwilling to do so.

Then, with the development of post-war town-planning large numbers of families moved away to new towns where there were no cinemas. Sometimes the planning authorities forgot to allocate a site for a cinema, but, when they did leave space for such amenities, the cost of the land and the expense of building a theatre made the cinema exhibitors hesitate to risk so much money to cater for a limited local audience. A number of young people in Britain have grown up in districts which have no cinema and they only see films when they are transmitted on a television screen.

The difficulties of getting to a cinema and the increased cost of public transport have made cinema audiences today more selective. Most people no longer go regularly once or twice a week to their

A scene from the Czech production Magic Lantern *which combines film and stage in one performance*

local cinema to sit in the same familiar seat. Now, they go only if they like the notices of the film and feel it is the sort of show they will enjoy and which will give a reward of pleasure for the effort of going. Otherwise, they stay at home and watch the television. This does not apply so much to young people, who enjoy going out and do not mind making an effort to obtain their entertainment. So more and more films are aimed at the under-twenty-fives. But even this age-group does not make a guaranteed audience, since there are many other things on which to spend the money they have for entertainment and relaxation, such as motor-cycles, dancing and long-playing records.

New Techniques

Long before the war, the film industry was aware of the need to keep reorganising itself so as to attract new audiences as well as to retain the interest of those it already had. In the world of entertainment nothing stands still. In the 1920's sound was introduced, and this gave film-going a tremendous fillip. In the 1930's colour was the craze, but it was nothing like as successful in attracting the public as sound had been. After the war all sorts of "stunts" were tried: 3-D (which was abandoned because the audience could not trouble to wear special glasses), wide screens, stereophonic sound; Todd-AO, Cinerama and many other devices to make the screen wider and larger and the sound more natural and dispersed round the theatre. One of the more recent novelties is the Czech entertainment, *Magic Lantern*, in which film and "trick-films" are blended with live action on the stage before the screen.

Types of films changed too. There was a spate of horror films which, for a time, attracted large numbers of people. Then there was a series of spectacles, reminiscent of films made before 1914. Larger and larger crowds of extras were employed and Old Testament history and chronicles of Rome and the Ancient World were ransacked for tales of luxury, crime and spectacle. These, too, attracted some patrons to the cinema, especially if the films were well acted and the scripts not too incredible—as some tended to be.

In the meantime, television was also having a beneficial effect on film producers. The entertainment value of some of the television plays with their small casts and simple settings was noted. Good television directors were attracted into the film industry and many simple, but highly successful films resulted.

As a result of the influence of television, cinema audiences have become more selective. There is a large part of the population that will make an effort to see a *good* film. The bush telegraph gets to work and people know that a certain picture is worth viewing and will join long queues to see it. Interestingly enough, such films with gripping, logical stories— films which are well acted and well produced—do not need any gimmicks or even colour to bring in their patrons. But third-rate films no longer attract the large audiences which poured into the cinemas in the early days.

One aspect of film production which has not survived the onslaught of television is the newsreel. In reporting news, the immediacy of television gives it a lead over any film, however rapidly it may be transported, processed and edited. If you can watch the Boat race while it is being rowed or see it re-rowed on video-tape a few hours later, a newsreel, even seen as early as the next afternoon, has still lost the quality of news. Most newsreels have been turned, with success, into film magazines, a reel of interesting items which do not pretend to report day-to-day events. The liveliness of television documentaries, with their interviews, has also influenced the film companies and tended to enliven film documentaries.

For authors, actors, technical workers and engineers, the coming of television has widely extended the spheres in which they can work. However, television, in which an actor appears before one or two people in their own home, requires a very different technique from film, in which the actor may be playing to an audience of two thousand, or a live theatre, where he has no help from a microphone.

Direction of television differs from film direction because it demands speed of thought and immediate decisions. Camera-work is different because of the perpetual movement in the television studio, the different shape of the screen and its small size, on which perhaps no more than three characters can appear with advantage. The smallness of the screen and the quality of the lighting influence the designer and, since the engineers want varying degrees of black and grey for good transmission, he is faced with a need to introduce variety of colour and of patterned material into his blue-prints without their appearing fussy.

The Audience

Television has influenced the attitudes of audiences as much as it has affected the film industry and the production teams.

People who can turn on their entertainment and then ignore it or talk through it, soon lose their powers of appreciation and discrimination unless they make an effort to retain them. In the cinema, the audience around you soon protests if you talk, turn your back on the screen, or get up out of your seat in the middle of the film.

At home, looking at the television, you must discipline yourself into being a good viewer. We have come a long way since the time when cave-men drew magic pictures into which they tried to introduce the illusion of movement—and since the dancing firelight or torchlight made such pictures seem to move. We have come a long way in our inventions, which have made moving, talking pictures available in our homes at the flick of an electric switch. But it is for us, each one of us, to make sure that our sense of appreciation and discrimination as we watch is as far ahead of the cave-man's as our television is ahead of his crude paintings on the cave wall.

An orchestra of 110 players records the musical score for Cinerama's Search for Paradise. *Dimitri Tiomkin leads the orchestra in his music while co-ordinating it with the action on the curved screen*